THE POLITICAL ROLE

OF LABOR

IN DEVELOPING COUNTRIES

by BRUCE H. MILLEN

31820

The Brookings Institution
Washington, D.C.

THE BROOKINGS INSTITUTION is an independent organization devoted to nonpartisan research, education, and publication in economics, government, foreign policy, and the social sciences generally. Its principal purposes are to aid in the development of sound public policies and to promote public understanding of issues of national importance. The Institution was founded December 8, 1927, to merge the activities of the Institute for Government Research, founded in 1916, the Institute of Economics, founded in 1922, and the Robert Brookings Graduate School of Economics and Government, founded in 1924.

The general administration of the Institution is the responsibility of a self-perpetuating Board of Trustees. The Trustees are likewise charged with maintaining the independence of the staff and fostering the most favorable conditions for creative research and education. The immediate direction of the policies, program, and staff of the Institution is vested in the President, assisted by the division directors and an advisory council, chosen from the professional staff of the Institution.

In publishing a study, the Institution presents it as a competent treatment of a subject worthy of public consideration. The interpretations and conclusions in such publications are those of the author or authors and do not purport to represent the views of the other staff members, officers, or trustees of the Brookings Institution.

Foreword

THE LABOR MOVEMENTS of the emerging countries are concerned
with far more than immediate "bread-and-butter" unionism, for they
are also involved—sometimes deeply—in playing a role on the political
scene. This has posed serious questions not only for the United States
government but for the American labor movement and other nongov-
ernmental groups concerned with the future of the developing countries.

Americans, accustomed to a relatively different pattern of labor activity, have found it difficult to understand this political role, to decide
what policies should govern United States attitudes toward it, and to
determine what practical measures would best assist the development
of a stable trade unionism in the new states. There has been a tendency
among students of the labor problems of various Latin American, African, and Asian countries to give the political aspect little more than
peripheral attention, concentrating primarily on economic and social
questions, and, to the extent they have treated the political issues, to
do so primarily in accordance with United States traditions and values.

The purpose of the present study is to focus directly on the political
policies and functions of organized labor in the emerging nations of
Africa and Asia, with particular emphasis on implications for United
States policy. The project was originally designed by Ben S. Stephansky,
former labor adviser in the Bureau of Inter-American Affairs of the
U. S. Department of State and presently United States Ambassador to
Bolivia, and Philip M. Kaiser, former Assistant Secretary of Labor for
International Affairs and presently United States Ambassador to Sene-
gal, in consultation with H. Field Haviland, Jr., Director of Foreign
Policy Studies of the Brookings Institution. The study was started in
the fall of 1960 with Mr. Stephansky as principal author and Mr.
Kaiser as his collaborator. Mr. Stephansky had been granted leave by
the Department of State to undertake the study as a Federal Executive
Fellow under the Advanced Study Program of the Brookings Institution.

When the two authors received ambassadorial appointments in the
spring of 1961, Bruce H. Millen, then labor adviser in the Bureau of
Near Eastern and South Asian Affairs of the Department of State and

since the fall of 1962 labor attaché in the United States Embassy in India, agreed to undertake the project and was granted leave for this purpose. Because there had been opportunity for little more than preparatory research when he assumed the task, he was responsible for most of the research and all of the writing. Mr. Millen has done graduate work in labor affairs and economics at the University of Wisconsin. From 1946 to 1951 he worked in various capacities with the Congress of Industrial Organizations; since 1951 he has been a labor specialist in the Department of State, his concerns including Italy and Norway as well as the Middle East and South Asia.

The study was done under the general supervision of Mr. Haviland and Robert E. Asher, member of the Brookings Senior Staff, and, in accordance with the usual Brookings practice, the author had the benefit of consultation with an advisory committee of leading specialists. The committee members were: Mr. Asher; Lewis Carliner, United Auto Workers; John Dunlop, Professor of Economics, Harvard University; Joseph LaPalombara, Professor of Political Science, Michigan State University; George Lichtblau, Department of State; Oliver A. Peterson, Visiting Professor of International Labor Studies, American University; Morris Weisz, Deputy Assistant Secretary of Labor and Adjunct Professor of International Labor Relations, American University; and John P. Windmuller, Professor of Industrial and Labor Relations, Cornell University. Mr. Lichtblau also prepared a background paper for the study. The author and the Institution are indebted to this group for their thoughtful comments and constructive suggestions.

The Institution is grateful to the Rockefeller Foundation for providing most of the funds necessary to finance the project.

The views expressed are the author's and do not purport to represent those of the consultants, or of the trustees, officers, or other staff members of the Brookings Institution.

ROBERT D. CALKINS
President

February 1963

Author's Acknowledgments

THERE ARE MANY PEOPLE to whom I am indebted for assistance prior to and during the preparation of this study. Notably included among them are the members of my advisory committee, named in the Foreword, who individually and collectively helped to spark ideas and at times demurred at certain trial balloons that might have carried me too far off course. There are also the members of the Research Seminar on Comparative Labor Movements, under the chairmanship of Everett M. Kassalow, Director of Research, Industrial Union Department, AFL-CIO; it was at meetings of the Seminar, which is sponsored by the National Institute of Labor Education, that many of the ideas contained in this book were first discussed and treated to informed inquiry.

I am especially grateful for the in-house guidance and encouragement that H. Field Haviland and Robert E. Asher of the Brookings Institution always gave willingly to an often troubled author. Clare Belman, my research assistant, not only kept me supplied with accurate background facts and figures but also put many an idea in the hopper. Kathleen Sproul, editorial associate at Brookings, applied skill and many long hours to seeing the manuscript through to publication. Susan Ewell, Harriet Daum, Alace Harvey, Carole DuPré, and Eleanor Rabbitt were among the succession of typists and secretaries who worked on numerous drafts of the manuscript without complaint.

My thanks are also due three institutions: the Department of State, which permitted me the time to produce the study; the Rockefeller Foundation, which made funds available to the Brookings Institution for the necessary research and travel; and finally to Brookings itself, which provided an atmosphere of such friendly cooperation that my months in working residence there will remain in mind as one of the high points of my life.

BRUCE MILLEN

Contents

The Political Role of Labor
in Developing Countries

CHAPTER ONE

Introduction

THE TERM "TRADE UNIONISM" traditionally ascribes to worker organizations a particular philosophy and function—collective representation to protect and advance the interests of the worker as a producer within the economic system. This is the core around which nearly all labor movements have been built from the eighteenth century to the present. In practice, the predominance of the economic motif has varied, most commonly in proportion to an organization's political involvement.

The wide range of present patterns includes the classic three-part alliances within a number of European movements—trade union, political party, consumer cooperative; the virtually unique persistence of economic unionism within the American labor movement, where political action is indirect and usually employed only as an extension of the economic function; and the intense and consistent "political unionism" in which the trade unions of most of the developing countries are now involved, to a degree that often seems to obscure the economic base.[1]

Each of these variations of course relates in part to the pattern of its environment. For the long-established labor movements of Europe and the United States, the story is fairly well known. It is clear, for example, that the relatively apolitical model seen in the United States was the admission price demanded of the movement by nineteenth century society. To Americans, less accustomed than Europeans to multiple and diverse political currents, the political ferment that

[1] Throughout this book, the term "trade union" is used generically to refer to the entire range of labor organizations—federations of labor (or national centers), national and local unions, and district councils. The functions analyzed are, for the most part, those of the federations in various of the new countries. The behavior patterns of the subgroups are not too different from those of a federation, although local unions are faced more directly with worker demands.

played some part in the early struggles of the unions for recognition was highly suspect, especially when for a time it included radical theories imported from Europe. The few unions that attempted to be, or to affiliate with, political parties eventually collapsed.

The "job-conscious" pattern turned out to be a very successful one for the American labor movement. The concept has been fairly elastic, and in recent years a number of unions have interpreted their role very broadly. But by and large the energies of the union leader have been concentrated on the job of collective bargaining, "and there the very logic of his position—in an economy where economic decisions are decentralized—is to pursue the special interests of his constituents."[2]

This image of a successful labor movement that does not involve itself directly in the "politics" of the political system has in general been firmly accepted by the American public of the twentieth century and, at least until very recently, by a majority of the labor specialists in the universities and in the government. The conception is broadly accurate, but does not take into account important nuances that have often been unnoted or misread. Especially, as I see it, are the words "political" and "economic" construed too narrowly in this context, for trade unions are by nature highly political organizations.

The rights that permit them to exist as legal entities, to organize, and to achieve their stated economic goals were originally won from a reluctant political status quo. Actions taken by the executive, legislative, judicial branches of a government determine in great part the role unions are to play. Lacking governmental sanction, they may become clandestine, semi-subversive organizations, but when they are enfranchised within the system of countervailing power they may have great value as a stabilizing force. In any case, they are part of the political rubric of a society, and political importance and often political power accrue to labor leaders because of their ready access to and influence over great numbers of people.

These political facts of life are better understood in Europe, where the range of union types is wide, than in the United States, and they are also understood by most of the political leaders and the union leaders who are working together as political partners in the developing countries. Americans are aware, because writers on international labor affairs have told them so, that nearly all labor movements overseas tend to emphasize political action. The tendency is usually deplored, and its origin and meaning are not much pondered.

[2] William Gomberg, "The Future of Collective Bargaining," *The Nation*, Vol. 194 (Jan. 20, 1962), p. 59.

Prior to World War II, the rapport of European labor with American labor was disturbed by the tendency of the Americans to see their union pattern as the normal one—and all others as aberrations or perhaps the product of sinister forces. This same viewpoint is now complicating American relationships with labor movements in the developing countries of Africa and Asia. There, as in other emerging countries, trade unions have sprung into active political participation; the significance of this to the total political development of new national entities has more often than not been overlooked or misinterpreted by the American observers and labor advisers who are concerned in the effort to encourage and strengthen the development of trade unionism as a stabilizing force in the new nations.

This study was originally conceived because a number of labor specialists who are interested in the institutional evolution of labor movements, as such, wanted to know more about the circumstances that have made "political unionism" thrive consistently and intensively in these countries. It seemed clear that looking askance at political unionism would provide no answers. Whether or not the relationships between labor leaders and political leaders are palatable to western observers, the dynamics of the situation demand that they be better understood.

This book, then, is an attempt to describe and interpret these political partnerships. I hope it will shed light on the present course of unionism in the developing countries, and by so doing suggest what further courses may be feasible as national development progresses. The quest for information about the events, processes, and attitudes that need to be better understood included both first-hand observation and a fairly intensive review of the available literature. The analysis was designed to examine (1) the factors—social, economic, political— that have influenced the main direction of labor activity in Asia and Africa; (2) how the union leaders go about their political functions and to what extent they are or are not neglecting the economic functions; and (3) what value, if any, the labor movements have to the society other than as mass organizations which helped to win independence. The chief points of reference are situations in Africa and Asia, since these are best known to me through recent experience, but past and present situations in a number of other countries are also discussed, because the nature of the study necessitated a concern with the entire question of union involvement in politics.

The Problem

At the close of World War II, scores of American trade union leaders and government labor specialists were called to Germany and Japan by the United States military administrations. It was believed that the labor movements of both countries had a vital part to play in economic and social recovery; however, they obviously needed help during the period when they were emerging from the general debacle and trauma of defeat and relearning the idiom of democratic institutions.

This project foreshadowed the policy that was soon to become part of the federal government's foreign aid program. Under the Truman Doctrine of 1947, similar assistance was given to labor movements in Greece and became as well a facet of the Economic Cooperation Administration's plans for European recovery. Somewhat later the range of the policy included the developing countries of Latin America, Asia, and Africa. Specific projects have been conducted variously and cooperatively by advisers from government agencies, labor organizations, and a number of universities, and the labor groups have also sponsored programs of their own. The activity has been extensive and intensive, not only in the countries being assisted, but also in the United States, where in recent years, as many as 900 foreign labor leaders and government officials concerned with labor affairs have annually been visitors, under the auspices of the Departments of State and Labor and the economic aid agencies.

The policy under which the programs operate has been expressed in a number of the statutes whereby Congress approved it, but perhaps most clearly in the Moody-Benton "Free Enterprise" amendment to the Mutual Security Act of 1951:

Sec. 516. It is hereby declared to be the policy of the Congress that this Act shall be administered in such a way as (1) to eliminate the barriers to, and provide the incentives for, a steadily increased participation of free private enterprise in developing the resources of foreign countries consistent with the policies of this Act, (2) to the extent that it is feasible and does not interfere with the achievement of the purposes set forth in this Act, to discourage the cartel and monopolistic business practices prevailing in certain countries receiving aid under this Act which result in restricting production and increasing prices, and to encourage where suitable competition and productivity, and (3) to encourage where suitable the development and strengthening of the free labor union movements as the collective bargaining agencies of labor within such countries.

During Senate debate on the original amendment, Senator William Benton summed up his reasons for sponsoring assistance to foreign labor movements:[3]

> . . . my suggested amendment has two parts. The second part deals with the urgent importance of administering [funds appropriated under the act] in such a way as to encourage the development of the free labor union movements of Europe as strong and influential agents of the working men and women . . . in their collective bargaining with their employers.
>
> The overwhelming dominance of Communist unions in France and Italy is not generally realized in the United States. Even less generally realized . . . is the fact that many of the dominant continental manufacturers would rather deal with the Communist unions than support and develop the free labor movement . . . [in the hope that] the Communist menace, at the psychological moment, will be met by a political swing to the . . . right. This hope induces . . . [the manufacturer] to run the grave risk to himself, as well as to his country, in preferring the short-term profit from his dealings with the Communist unions to the long-term political and economic stability which strong, free, independent labor movements, which place their reliance on collective bargaining rather than political pressures and shenanigans, can and would help develop.

The term "free and independent trade unionism," which thereafter became the policy beacon for both government and organized labor assistance to labor movements abroad has never been precisely defined, except as expressed in the Benton amendment. But in general it seems to imply a model of unionism that (1) is primarily, if not exclusively, concerned with the economic function of collective bargaining to win benefits for the worker, (2) is not linked with or/and controlled by a government or political party, (3) has no Communist connections.

The only labor movement in the world whose operations accord with all three of these specifications is that of the United States. Least of all does the model relate to the trade unions of Asia and Africa. Most of them are not at present primarily concerned with collective bargaining; most have strong political affiliations, and some are under government control; the majority of them are anti-Communist, but in the context of the cold war this is in itself a political stance, and one that involves many subtle problems. The "free and independent" slogan, as used

---

[3] *Congressional Record*, Vol. 97, Pt. 8 (Aug. 31, 1951), p. 10945. As originally framed by Senator Benton, the amendment referred specifically to European labor and did not include the first part of the present Section 516.

In a 1952 amendment (66 Stat. 150) to the Act, Congress authorized the expenditure of $100,000,000 to further the total objectives of Section 516.

by American union representatives and government officials alike, seems essentially a statement of faith and hope—faith in the democratic process as the United States knows it, and hope for the future of the new countries. Nevertheless, because the idea is based on assumptions that are not at present applicable to these countries, it has hampered our understanding of what is actually taking place there.

The primary assumption posits foreign unions as unfledged and rudimentary expressions of trade unionism as it is known in the United States. According to the American model, they are therefore expected to stress their "economic" function through more intensive efforts to bargain collectively with employers, and to make their "political" function less explicit and less direct—e.g., by supporting progressive parties and candidates instead of operating within a party structure. It is duly acknowledged in this view that a nation's social structure (and thereby its political structure) is stronger when it includes well-established unions; however, the strength is often mainly credited to their skill in winning benefits and security within the industrial setting. In other words, in the American context, well-stocked refrigerators, paid-up car and home ownership, and protected job rights will in themselves produce social harmony and hence constitute a barrier to subversive overtures. For the foreign scene, the security goals would be expressed more modestly but the principle would be the same.

Such assumptions are in part a reflection of the "American dream" —which has to a large extent become reality, thanks to the existence of certain characteristics in our political system which in the long run have permitted unions to win for their members benefits and security that in turn have contributed to political viability. But since these characteristics do not exist in the developing countries, I am convinced that the above assumptions are unwarranted in this frame of reference and, especially when combined with the unrealistic iteration of "free and independent," constitute an unreliable policy base for the job of encouraging unionism. Many of the programs resulting from this approach have fallen short of the mark, and some of them have come close to entirely defeating their own ends.

In one country, for example, advisers from an important segment of the American labor movement gave justifiable encouragement to a split in the general labor confederation that had become dominated by Communists—but thereafter all effort was concentrated on assisting the creation of a new apolitical, anti-Communist confederation. How an organization could be active as an anti-Communist force and apolitical at one and the same time was never made clear; the consequent confusion affected the local political situation adversely. In several other countries the American sponsors of a certain group of programs—aimed at diverting the unions from political activities—seemed to be hoping that such diversion would eventually lead to a break in their political affiliations, which in these cases were non-Communist. If this really was the objective, it was not achieved—and the programs had little other perceptible effect.

The continued attempt to deal with trade unionism in these countries as if it should have only indirect, if any, links with politics is a serious misinterpretation of the dynamics at work. Even more damaging, it also reduces the possibility of cooperation between the Americans and the indigenous labor leaders by emphasizing the existing conflict in points of view.

Although the total ramifications of the conflict are complicated, one basic difference can be simply expressed. American trade unions did not create the pluralistic society of the United States or its system of countervailing power, but they were able to win certain political and economic rights that permitted them to become part of the system. From that stance, their activities in behalf of their members continued to contribute to the kind of social change that leads to further political stability. Thus, American labor and political leaders tend to believe that the indirect economic and social pressures generated by the establishment of well-organized collective bargaining units are the precursors of political change.[4]

Their Asian and African counterparts in the emerging countries sense that, for them, political change is a prerequisite to economic and social change. The more sophisticated among the labor leaders are fully aware that labor movements, if isolated from political relationships of any sort, are primarily reactive instruments. And they know

[4] One U. S. labor leader on returning from a visit to India suggested that the problem of "bucking-up" the Indian trade unions had an easy solution: just send in, en masse, 100 experienced American organizers. He had apparently forgotten a lesson that should have been learned from American labor's own abortive attempt to organize the southern part of the United States after World War II. Many union officials had believed that success in establishing collective bargaining units throughout the Deep South would lead, over time, to dramatic political changes. The effort was resolute; at one time, for example, more than 300 CIO organizers were in the field. But the truth of the matter was simply this: the hostility of the existing political forces in the region had from the outset precluded extensive organization.

that "pure" trade unions do not write the book of politics; a powerful labor organization can influence events in many ways, but the major decisions are made elsewhere. Thus it is understandable that union leaders in these countries—where the political situation is extremely fluid and the possibility exists of influencing the nature of the society that is to evolve—consider it desirable, and even necessary, to have political affiliations.

Not all the union movements associated with a political force in either Africa or Asia are initiators in their own right, and those which become completely dominated by a party or are restrained by rigid government controls are sometimes pathetic, feeble instruments. Yet even under such circumstances a union leader usually will not forsake his commitments to the goals of the regime and will continue to see himself as contributing to the total movement of national development. In exchange for loyalty to the political movement, however, he may also hope to extract some small gains for his union's membership and to improve his personal power position within the political structure.

"Political Unionism" Defined

The term "political unionism" is subject to a variety of interpretations, since most labor organizations, including those in the United States, engage in political activity. It is necessary, therefore, to differentiate between the "economic union" that is to some degree involved in politics and the "political union" that carries on economic functions, but may subordinate them.

The political approach of American unions, as noted earlier, is usually an extension of their economic function. Legislation related to the membership's interests as workers, consumers, or taxpayers will be supported, and candidates who favor the type of legislation wanted by the unions will be backed. Progressive legislation—such as aid to education—which has an impact beyond their own membership is also generally supported. With few exceptions, American labor leaders have employed the established political channels, and although a rally might be staged, for instance, in favor of a medical aid bill that is being debated by Congress, a strike would never be called for this purpose. In England, the trade unions are much more directly involved in politics through participation in the Labor Party, but, here too, much of the involvement is pointed toward goals more or less related to the traditional functions of economic unionism.

As I define it, the "political union" has certain specific characteristics:

1. The amount of time and thought invested in direct political work is a primary index. The political union's leaders are directly engaged in political operations and discussions day in and day out.

2. The goals of its leadership are very broad, in contrast to the usually circumscribed goals of union leaders in the United States, and may include revamping the major rules governing the society. The political union, through its support of "open-end" objectives, seeks improved living standards for its members, but may temporarily be willing to go slow in achieving them in the hope of winning political power.

3. The frequent use of direct mass action—a demonstration, a strike, or sometimes a staged riot—in support of nonindustrial objectives, and a propensity for tailoring the performance of economic functions to serve political ends are constant factors. Protest is almost never registered through as mild a method as a "write-letters-to-Congress" campaign that unions in the United States might mount.

4. Ideological conformity in the leadership is required, although the tolerable limits of dissent may vary. Communist labor movements are the most demanding, nationalist movements somewhat less so. Movements that are linked only loosely to a party or government are usually permissive, demanding only general support of the ideology.

5. There is a marked tendency toward "movementism"—i.e., the continual determination to form or participate in a broad-based political force aimed at capturing and maintaining political power. Trade unionism alone is considered an inadequate instrument with which to attain the political, economic, and social reforms sought by the union leaders.

There are, however, exceptions to the movement tendency, especially in certain Middle East countries where the political elites have, for the most part, attempted to control the labor groups instead of including them in a mass front. As a consequence, the union leadership is likely to engage in maneuvers that are still highly political but uninspired by an ideology.

6. In the early stages of a movement-building process, a political union often closely resembles a political party—and may indeed be a party. Eventually, however, the many problems encountered in the

wider interest-spectrum of a party tend to press the union back to its specialized area of labor representation. But even here the interests it looks after are not only those of its own often small and unstable membership but also the broader ones of an idealized national labor force.

"Political unionism" and "economic unionism" are clearly not mutually exclusive means of action but two facets of the organized labor pattern, which often may alternate in the operations of a given union. In the operations of most Asian and African unions the political facet is durably and highly visible—much more so than in the unions of the developed countries—but blendings are found. A Ceylonese labor leader (who also headed a political party) described this to a group in Washington some years ago: "It is true that political leaders like myself originally got into the trade union field to strengthen the nationalist effort— but this did not mean that we were free to ignore the workers' job-related demands. We had to get something for them in order to hold their loyalty."

The characteristics of "political unionism" as stated above apply in general to the organizations that are the concern of this book. Yet it is necessary to remember that every organization mentioned here is fundamentally only representative of itself. It has always been impossible to encompass within any single term or phrase what it is that constitutes a "labor organization." Robert Franklin Hoxie spelled out the difficulty many years ago:

> The union program, taking it with all its mutations and contradictions, comprehends nothing less than all the various economic, political, ethical, and social viewpoints and modes of action of a vast and heterogeneous complex of working-class groups, molded by diverse environments and actuated by diverse motives.[5]

A labor organization is made up of human beings and is responsive to a wide array of problems sensed and felt. Thus each one, whether local union or national center, is unique. Moreover, there is a constant flux as the union acts and reacts to changing internal and external developments, so that the union of tomorrow is likely to be something different from the union of today.

In presenting a generalized picture, then, one runs the risk of oversimplifying or of overlooking important characteristics of labor or-

---

[5] Robert Franklin Hoxie, *Trade Unionism in the United States* (Appleton, 1922), p. 35.

ganizations in an individual country. The wide range of union function and operation in any given country is difficult to span: describing an American union such as the United Auto Workers provides but little insight into the National Maritime Union or any of the unions of the construction trades; so, too, in Kenya, the characteristics of the Mombasa Port Workers Union are quite different from those of the General Agricultural Workers Union. But Kenya unions as a whole differ from United States unions more than they differ from each other—and that is the point this study is trying to make.

Types and Functions

Bearing in mind the caveat above—that each organization described in these pages is representative only of itself—it may nevertheless be useful to offer here a spectrum of categories into which the unions of various countries can be grouped. The categories necessarily overlap, and the situations in the developing countries are still so fluid that the characteristics of any union may change rapidly. However, the groupings will indicate wherein the present unionism of the new countries differs from or corresponds to that of older countries. The relation of political setting to the group characteristics briefly stated here is discussed more fully in Chapter Three.

• The unionism exemplified by the United States model is at one extreme of the spectrum, that of the Soviet bloc at the other. As pointed out earlier, the dominant note in the American labor movement is the collective bargaining function, although political action in some sense of the term has always been included in union programs. American unions are by tradition free and independent of government and political parties. Historically, especially during the early stages of labor organization, strong controls were at times exerted on union activity, but in the main by private employers, who were, however, often supported by judicial interpretation or administrative action of public authorities.

• Next on the spectrum are the unions of the North European countries—typified by those of Scandinavia. Collective bargaining and economic action rank high on their list of priorities, and functional links with Social Democratic and Labor parties are usual. Many of the organizations have engaged in direct political strikes, but as they acquired political responsibility such activities became more rare.

Although the unions cooperate closely with political parties and formulate wage policy in keeping with party objectives, they have an independent source of power, and can, therefore, be considered "free and independent." Obviously, however, to apply the phrase here supplements its American connotation.

• Because Israel is in many respects unique, it belongs in a class by itself. Although Histadrut, the labor federation, relates somewhat to the North European category in its basic socialist ideology, the addition of Zionism and nationalism has imparted special characteristics and given it a "nation-building" philosophy. Histadrut is as much an expression of political drive as it is of trade unionism; links with political parties are close and for the most part mutually beneficial. Collective bargaining has been a commonly used tool but is not dominant. Because of its political ties, Histadrut is of course not free and independent in the American sense of the term, but because it is itself a power center within the complicated party structure, it is not a captive—and is certainly philosophically closer to the American model than to the Russian.

• The next point on the spectrum can be represented by Italy or France—or India and Ceylon.[6] The dominance of ideological concepts here is the basis of highly politicized trade unionism carried on within the framework of a competitive political system. There is a history of left-wing radicalism, including revolutionary socialism and communism, and the general or industry-wide strike for the attainment of economic and political purposes is still retained as a weapon. Union ties with political parties are the norm and permit, in varying degrees, party influence on trade union matters. The extent of independent power retained by the unions is a variable not only from country to country of this category but also within each of the countries, depend-

---

[6] Many of the Latin American and Caribbean countries would also seem to fit into this general category, according to discussions I have had with trade union and political leaders from this region. Too, Robert J. Alexander's description of Latin American labor as one of the revolutionary forces and "an integral part of the revolt against the traditional society" has a familiar ring. ("Organized Labor and the Bolivian National Revolution," paper presented to the Research Seminar on Comparative Labor Movements, Washington, D.C., 1962. This paper and nine others by Seminar members will be included in a book to be published by Northwestern University Press in mid-1963: National Labor Movements in the Postwar World, edited by Everett M. Kassalow.) George I. Blanksten's comment that Latin American labor articulates the views of large numbers who are otherwise unrepresented in the interest-group structure also matches the picture. (See "Latin America," in Gabriel A. Almond and James S. Coleman, eds., The Politics of the Developing Areas, Princeton University Press, 1960, p. 512.)

ing upon which union-party relationship, among the several within the open system, is being examined.

• In the Middle East grouping (Israel aside) the labor organizations, with the exception of those in Lebanon, are or have been subject to stern control by the respective governments. As noted earlier, they tend therefore to be the "political-maneuver" type. The Turkish unions have been gradually gaining additional rights recently, but still fall far short of being free or independent. Collective bargaining is limited by both the nature of the economy and the restraints imposed by government. The unions in Egypt have been striving for something more substantive, but the government's ambivalence in seeking to build a mass political organization and at the same time maintain close watch over the component units has so far restricted them to this grouping.

• In Africa, many of the unions might properly be grouped under the general heading of "political-maneuver" and controlled organizations, although the degree of restraint is probably somewhat less than that exercised by Middle East governments. In countries that are guided in part by conservative remnants of the old *patrone* parties, the unions are generally expected to play a modest role, or none at all; the labor movements of Liberia, Dahomey, the Ivory Coast, and, possibly, Sierra Leone are illustrative of this. (In Sierra Leone there has been some evidence that changes are taking place.) The organizations do have a modicum of internal autonomy, but if they try to follow an independent course they have relatively little importance and are subject to controls.

In some of the African countries, however, a more dynamic type of union is dominant. These are the countries where the mass, structured party is in control or where there is evidence that a move in this direction is in process: Algeria, Tunisia, Guinea, Ghana, Tanganyika, Kenya, and, possibly, Senegal are representative. The labor movements here are highly political and, in the first four countries named, are also attempting to play a large political role. Although collective bargaining is not characteristically emphasized, it is not neglected. Most of the organizations are now coming under increasing government control, but because their operations are dynamic and because they give active support to government programs they have retained a voice in high councils and varying amounts of influence on over-all policy. The most extreme examples in this grouping—Ghana and Guinea—are much closer on the spectrum to the Russian model than to that of the United States.

• Finally, of course, we reach the Soviet trade union system, in which I include the systems of all countries within the Sino-Soviet bloc. Collective bargaining is clearly subservient to the goals of the state, the trade unions are clearly subordinated to the Communist Party, and the question of union autonomy is irrelevant. The unions have been agents of the state since 1928, when Tomsky was replaced as head of the union federation by Kaganovitch as a consequence of the decision to force the unions to be production-minded rather than consumption-minded.

The rapidity of change in the developing countries makes it virtually certain that the above groupings will not remain static, but as of the summer of 1962 they appeared to be relevant to the situations observed.

Involved in the problem of rapid change, and making political unionism even more difficult to understand, is the shift in role when the labor arm of a political force moves from its pre-independence opposition to the colonial government to post-independence responsibility for cooperating with the new government. This shift has been especially common in much of Africa, where there are also assorted variations of it to add to our confusion. The case of the Union Marocaine du Travail in Morocco is one variation: the highly nationalistic UMT moved into opposition after liberation; the oppositional course, however, has been more restrained than that taken prior to independence. There is also a distinction in role for unions operating under the one-party systems common to Africa, and those under multiple-party systems, as in India and Ceylon, where the observer encounters the many puzzling problems of competitive unionism. And all of this must be traced within the context of a fluid political situation.

Melding of Traditional and Modern Forms

All in all, what is known about both the politics and the job-oriented work of labor organizations in the new countries is insignificant to what still needs to be learned. The melding of pre-colonial instruments of social control and political management with new and western-inspired political structures and concepts is a subtle process, extremely difficult to define let alone understand.

Western observers may well feel thwarted in trying to probe the inner workings of an organization that is designated by the modern term "trade union" and composed of members and leaders still tied in large part to an economic system and a value system that date back hundreds, possibly thousands, of years. An anthropologist points out that "the behavioral traits associated with extended family groupings may be carried over and modified in the industrial setting with curious results."[7] There is ample evidence, for example, that the hiring and placement practices of many firms in Africa are tied to tribal and kinship relationships, if for no other purpose than to solve the problem of communication on the job, but we have no clues as to what such practices mean in terms of union structure and function. Presumably, they would work against building union solidarity, and they are certainly among the reasons why "the impersonal and standardized practices associated with large-scale trade unionism are difficult to introduce."[8]

There is probably no way to estimate precisely the part played by tradition and symbolism in the building of modern institutions. When one reads that Olujimi Ayodele Fagbenro Beyioku, a leader of the Nigerian Trade Union Congress, continues to carry the title "Chief," does this mean that his organization is not as modern as its name? Or does it mean that there has been a skillful regrouping of traditional controlling mechanisms in a new setting? The President of Guinea, Sékou Touré, was earlier the head of a trade union federation; he is also the grandson of Almamy Samory, a famous and powerful leader of two generations ago. It is quite likely, therefore, that traditionalism and modernism overlapped as factors in Touré's rise to power.

Recently, a group of visiting foreign union officials were guests at an American labor conference. One of the Africans wore a handsome headdress that provoked interested comment among the Americans. Someone surmised that it was a warrior's hat, possibly presented as part of the ritual marking transition to manhood. According to the wearer, this was partly correct. It was a warrior's hat, all right—presented to him by the membership of his union for his skill and courage in beating down a raid on the union by a rival group.

[7] Sidney W. Mintz, "Cultural Barriers Affecting International Labor Training in the United States," address to Conference on International Labor Training, American University, Washington, D.C., April 6-7, 1962 (mimeographed).
[8] *Ibid.*

Factors such as these—Beyioku's title, Touré's grandfather, and the warrior's hat—are not easy for the westerner to understand in relation to his earlier knowledge of unionism. Yet essentially they are not too different from kinship and status motifs in the West, even though we have discarded the epithet "tribal." It occurs to me that they are also ingredients of the concept "political" in its most significant sense, and if so, certainly add one more facet to the broad spectrum of political situations to be explored here.

In the wide range of union function and operation in the new countries of Africa and Asia and the greatly varied influences of different cultures and customs, there appears to be at least one common denominator: each labor movement operates within an ambiance that encourages political unionism of some sort and degree. The chapters to follow deal with the political, economic, and social factors that are, in part, the root cause of this type of unionism. Chapters Two through Six describe and analyze the characteristics, operations, and objectives of the unions; Chapters Seven and Eight attempt to evaluate specific aspects of labor's political alliance. In the final chapter, certain implications of the study are highlighted.

CHAPTER TWO

The New Unions in Profile

A FEW YEARS AGO I heard an Indonesian labor leader of consequence describe his initiation into unionism as follows: "When I was first sent into the railway shops to organize, I did not even know what a trade union was. We had been sent in to accomplish a para-military mission in the nationalist struggle against the Dutch. It was only later that I learned of collective bargaining." With a leadership so uninformed, one can surmise how long it took the railway rank and file to discover what their so-called organization was all about.

It is the intention of this study to describe and analyze the factors which have influenced the main direction of organized labor activity in the developing countries. But the factors cannot be seen in proper perspective unless it is first firmly established that the "physical" picture of the groups we are here dealing with is a far cry from the strongly entrenched, systematized union structure familiar to westerners. According to the present bench marks of organized labor in the United States, these unions appear sorely deficient. They are often amorphous and fragmented; a common structure is hard to discern; membership ties are uncertain and fragile; the labor contract in our sense is rare; and the leadership is, by and large, a patchwork of puzzling influences.

A composite profile based on some assembled evidence of these and other characteristics is offered below. Whether the characteristics, in sum, can accurately be said to mean that the labor movements of the new countries are deficient in function, in relation to their environment and when compared to the earliest movements in the now developed countries, will be considered at the end of the chapter and in chapters that follow.

Amorphousness

On first visiting a trade union in Asia and Africa a westerner is likely to ask himself: Where are the members? Where is the organization? All that he can see is a tiny, scantily equipped office, an officer or two, and possibly a clerk. There seem to be no regular meetings of the membership in a given plant, no shop stewards who might serve as a line of communication with the officers. There may be a large headquarters building to house the confederation of trade unions, as in Nairobi, Accra, and Casablanca, but the ties between the confederation and its affiliates and downward to the membership are not easily discernible. The organization appears to be all head and no body. Further study may reveal a series of executive organs at various levels, but these again seem to be representative of no one in particular.

In a good many instances the men who stand at the top of the structure are self-appointed spokesmen for a membership which is at best only partially committed in its loyalties to the union. This does not mean that the officer is without influence or that his power is based on a fiction, but it does indicate that these trade unions lack the definitive qualities of firmly established labor organizations in American terms. In part, it is this amorphous quality—this difficulty in locating an identifiable group of men composing a given organization—that has interfered with our understanding of the role of the union in the new societies.

In no one of the developing countries do the trade unions represent more than a small percentage either of the total population or of those who are working for wages. India is probably the most industrially advanced nation considered in these pages; its first national labor center was formed in 1920. Yet in 1958, Indian unions could claim as members only about 3 million workers out of a non-agricultural labor force of something under 40 million, or substantially less than 10 percent. This is explained in part by the fact that only about 7 million people work under conditions which lend themselves to organization.

In Ceylon, because of the extent of organization among plantation workers, the proportion of union membership is much higher—an estimated 32 percent of the wage-earning force.[1] Much of the economic

---

[1] U. S. Bureau of Labor Statistics, Division of Foreign Labor Conditions, *Labor Law and Practice in Ceylon* (April 1962; manuscript), p. 56.

bargaining power of the unions is lost, however, through the high degree of fragmentation. In 1960 there were 7 federations and 3 major omnibus unions; in all, there were 900 registered unions, which claimed a membership of something over 700,000.[2]

In Ghana, approximately 319,000 workers were in the recorded urban force in 1959—only 5 percent of the population.[3] The Ghana Trade Union Congress (TUC), however, was able to make a claim of over 500,000 members because the roster included agricultural workers, as the result of a compulsory membership feature in a 1958 amendment to the Industrial Relations Act. In Kenya the federation of labor claimed a membership in 1958 of 45,000, somewhat less than 9 percent of the employed labor force, enrolled in 42 registered unions.[4] The Moroccan Union Marocaine du Travail (UMT) is the only organization in Africa that can support a claim of a massive voluntary membership.

Fragmentation

The fragmentation of the labor movement in Ceylon, noted above, is a characteristic in all the countries where there is competition in the political field. In India, for example, there are four federations—all organized on the basis of ideology—plus thousands of small "independent" unions. Many of the latter are company dominated; others are Communist controlled, and still others are organized under the personal leadership of an individual political leader, who may be the actual or titular head of a half dozen local groups.

The Lebanese unions, where political play is more free than in other Middle East countries, are grouped in five federations. One is organized on a purely religious (Moslem) basis, one on an ideological basis (communism). The other three are anti-Communist, in large measure separated from each other only because of personality conflicts and political-power ambitions of individual leaders.

In Indonesia there are at least five federations of major or minor importance—all but one having in varying degrees ideological counterparts in the political sphere. Singapore has two major federations, plus

[2] *Ibid.*, pp. 56, 59.
[3] Ghana, Office of the Government Statistician, *Quarterly Digest of Statistics*, (Accra, September 1960), Table 3, p. 2.
[4] Colony and Protectorate of Kenya, *Labour Department Annual Report, 1959* (Nairobi, 1960), pp. 3, 13, and Appendix VIII, pp. 57-58.

some forty unions of governmental employees which have not committed themselves to either of the federations. Malaya is not plagued with multiple unionism, and up to 1962 the Malayan Trade Union Council (MTUC), composed of 80 affiliated unions with a combined membership of possibly 220,000, had "officially" eschewed political connections, although its leaders are either publicly identified with, or sympathetic to, the Socialist front parties.

In Africa, because the political situation generally tends toward one-party dominance, union centers are not so numerous. However, in Senegal, the Ivory Coast, and the Cameroun, multiple federations reflecting past international loyalties are tolerated.[5] These remaining splinter movements do not represent a political threat, and the respective governments are probably quite content to let the issue rest. In Nigeria the running fight between the Nigerian Trade Union Congress (NTUC) and the pro-western Trade Union Congress of Nigeria (TUCN) began to attract government attention in late 1961. There have been several abortive government-inspired attempts to merge the federations—the most recent in May 1962. The fragmented political structure, with three major parties each dominant in a single region, makes it difficult to bring order out of a chaotic situation.

As suggested above, some of the multiple unionism, particularly in the early stages of union and political development, has been a product of careerism and political factionalism under the aegis of individual politicians. But for the most part it reflects a factor that will be discussed in Chapter Three—that trade union splintering or consolidation is related to the development of political currents and agencies which exercise an influence over events in the labor field.

Lack of Structure

The variety of structural forms found among the labor organizations is a further source of confusion to the visiting observer. Craft unionism, generally the most stable structure and one that has formed the core of many union movements in the West, is not common here, in part because the guild system, which in western countries fed craft workers into the industrialization process, has in many of the new coun-

[5] The Senegalese UGTS (government-linked federation) and the Christian CNTCS merged in April 1962, forming the Union Nationale des Travailleurs Senegalais (UNTS).

tries stayed outside of the modern sector of the economy. However, that skilled groups were formerly imported also has bearing in this context. In Africa, for instance, the use of migrant labor, the preponderance of unskilled labor (which runs as high as 80 percent in Ghana), and the persisting control of skill jobs on the East Coast by Europeans and Asians, all continue to militate against the creation of an indigenous skill component of any significant size. The competition of low-paid unskilled workers erodes the skilled worker's position, putting less demand on his services and thereby reducing his bargaining power. Furthermore, the moving spirit behind organizational activity has been, and is, largely provided by politically oriented men—frequently with a Marxist background—who early determined against adoption of the craft form. The reason is obvious: once a craft union is stabilized it is usually concerned primarily with wages and hours and less with political change.

As might be expected in a poorly developed economy with limited communications, the earliest organizational form was the plant union (called "house union" in Africa), and there are now a myriad of these small one-plant groups in both Asia and Africa. The only organizations at all territorial in scope were the railway groups—since the enterprise itself spanned a large geographic area—and for this reason they have played a major part in the development of unionism and in the liberation movements.

Almost all of the single-plant unions lack the resources to do an effective job of collective bargaining, and many of them are company dominated. This type of organization frequently lends itself to Communist infiltration and control—often not so labeled. It may also become the personal instrument of a local political leader who fights off efforts to affiliate it with a larger body. In India there are reportedly some 4,000 to 5,000 of these small groups. Many of them have maintained their independence from national centers, but tend to be subject to rapid disintegration: 10 percent of the registered unions in India go under each year—often being replaced by equally fragile organizations.[6] This excessive fragmentation is partly traceable to colonial legislation still in force which permits as few as seven people to form a union.

Logically enough, given the relatively small industrial base, the first efforts to link the embryonic labor organizations in a coordinated

---

[6] *Indian Labor Year Book, 1953-54,* p. 148, cited by Charles A. Myers, in Walter Galenson, ed., *Labor and Economic Development* (Wiley, 1959), p. 37.

structure resulted in the development of "general" unions, which group all workers in one locale or region, regardless of trade or industry, into one organization. The form was particularly used in French West Africa. The general union is a sensible approach when local units would be excessively small; it happens also to lend itself to political manipulation, especially when the membership is largely unskilled and illiterate.

The trend in the early 1960's seemed to be toward the establishment of national federations of industrial or omnibus-type unions, in both South Asia and Africa. There are evident reasons for this: one, that as the countries develop union structure will have matched the industrial structure; another, that the present emphasis in all of these countries is on gaining some degree of control over trade union activities, sometimes in the interest of harnessing political power, sometimes simply to develop a more manageable type of organization responsive to "from-the-top-down" policy.

That the scattered "house unions" and even geographic general unions do not lend themselves to the type of controls now found necessary can be seen, for example, in Egypt and in Ghana, where recent legislation has prescribed government-authorized industrial unions and forced an amalgamation of existing units into them. Affiliation with the national center then became mandatory. The respective governments ran into strong opposition from organizations that did not want to lose their autonomy, and in both cases the number of authorized national unions was increased. In Ghana the number was increased from sixteen to twenty-four but later squeezed back to the original figure; in Egypt the implementation of the law was delayed for eighteen months until the government finally doubled the authorized total.

The move in India is toward the national industrial union, but, because of the country's size and the many linguistic and other divisions that exist, it may be that the state bodies will maintain their present dominance. The type of union within this structure, however, will no doubt be predominantly industrial or of the omnibus variety.

In Africa the trend is toward highly centralized federations to which the affiliates are responsible. This is in keeping with the centralizing tendencies in the political sphere. In Kenya, to cite one example, the secretary generals of both the Mombasa port workers union and the railway union were put into office by the federation, or more accurately by its secretary general. The port workers' officer was subsequently elected, and the railway man was to stand for election after he had matters under control. In India and Ceylon, the fragmented political structures work toward decentralization and a great deal of autonomy for affiliates of the respective national centers. This autonomy, once experienced, will not be surrendered easily.

The multiplicity of union federations and, in many of the countries, the as yet undetermined structure contribute to and are an index of the generally weak and untidy nature of the trade union scene. The organizations are not cohesive units whose policies and activities can be easily followed; the picture is blurred, defying easy compartmentalization. Membership figures are naturally inflated and cannot be readily verified. It is a floating membership, more often than not made up of followers and sympathizers who give their loyalty to the highest bidder, or to the political ideas articulated by the leadership. This is not necessarily an irrational procedure. Perhaps a man joins the Indian National Trade Union Congress (INTUC) to take advantage of certain bureaucratic or administrative privileges made available through that organization's political ties. At the same time he may align himself with the Communist All Indian Trade Union Congress (AITUC) because he feels a need to register a militant expression of protest across a broad range of social, political, and economic issues, often only indirectly related to the work life of the individual. In any case, it is a mistake for an observer to associate size of membership with influence, in view of the conditions faced by most of the unions in the new countries.

Financial Difficulties

Given the conditions under which the worker commits himself to participation in union affairs and given the major thrust of trade union interest, it is not surprising that the individual member rarely pays dues regularly. As a result, most of the unions are so poorly financed that they cannot afford full-time officers and staff members—which in turn makes it even more difficult to collect dues. Efforts to build a skilled cadre of leaders or carry out any program leading to the building of cohesive organizations are greatly hampered. When I was in Kenya in January 1962 the Kenya Federation of Labour (KFL), which is housed in a substantial modern headquarters built from funds donated primarily by American unions, had no telephone service because past telephone bills were so far in arrears. In India the national headquarters of the INTUC has been constantly pressed for funds, as have most of its regional affiliates; the Socialist federation, Hind Mazdoor Sabha (HMS), has been in even worse financial condition. Neither federation can support a publications program suited to its needs. The Trade Union Congress of Nigeria and many other African groups experience the same difficulties.

There are, however, a number of federations that are reasonably well off. The Moroccan UMT reportedly collects dues at least nine months out of twelve from 300,000 of a claimed membership of 576,000 members.[7] The organization owns real estate of considerable value, including a national headquarters building in Casablanca that is valuable also as a prestige symbol. The Ceylon Workers Congress (CWC) several years ago instituted a dues payment plan that is said to function effectively, and the Government Clerical Service Union in Ceylon also has a dues system, and operates a lottery as well.

The Ghana TUC has fairly adequate funds at its disposal because of the compulsory membership and compulsory dues systems enacted by the legislature. The National Union of Plantation Workers in Malaya has an efficient dues-stamp plan. The Bombay dock workers union gives every evidence of relative affluence, and one of its officers stated that a four-story office building completed in 1960 had been paid for through assessments on the membership. The Textile Labor Association in Ahmedabad—once under the stewardship of Gandhi—is outstanding in many respects. It has a large modern headquarters, 200 paid employees, and collects over $200,000 annually in dues from its membership of approximately 100,000. The Aden federation (ATUC), for years dependent on voluntary contributions from members only when negotiations or a strike had been successful, has finally regularized its financing.

Nevertheless, these more fortunate organizations are exceptions. The general pattern is financial dependency upon outside sources—government, political parties, philanthropists, private businessmen, individual politicians, and foreign or international labor movements. Unfortunately, the ease with which money can be raised from outside the country in the general context of the cold war discourages efforts to build dues programs. The financing in the early 1960's of the two rival trade union federations in Nigeria—one by the International Confederation of Free Trade Unions (ICFTU), the other by the Communists' World

Federation of Trade Unions (WFTU)—is a sample of the cold war's impact in the trade union sphere.

Dependence upon sources outside the union movement often leads to the compromising of principles and sometimes to actual corruption; it can also produce a certain type of careerism and lead to the establishment of "paper" unions. A good many American unions are beset by fund requests from shrewd operators long on promises to be anti-Communist and short on zeal. There is also a type of corruption of the mind that frequently overtakes those who aid the foreign unions, when merely by virtue of their gifts they feel that they have demonstrated their superior wisdom and acquired the right to exert influence.

The serious problem of dues collection is of course partly related to the fact that union objectives have been centered, at least until recently, not on building organizations but on mobilizing the masses for political action. The Moroccan UMT is an exception to this pattern, and demonstrates the value of developing a core group as a solid dues-paying base from which to carry on the more general objectives in the political field. Most of the organizations have not been able to achieve this goal; for those in a competitive union situation, particularly when a Communist union is part of the competition, the pressure is on to forgo incidental money matters in the interests of winning support for the political concepts represented by the party to which any given union is related. The Communist unions are usually well financed through the local Communist party or from foreign sources, and they must be combatted. The dues paid by a small membership are relatively of little value to a non-Communist union, when an essential part of its function, in the context of the ideological struggles that have been going on in so many of the new nations, is to serve as a propaganda agent in support of an ideology.

The dues problem is also closely related to another characteristic of the new unions. Most of them have come into being before the work force was structured, before industrial skills were widely known, and before any substantial part of the labor force was committed to industrial employment and urban living. As a result, the idea of identification with and loyalty to a labor organization is still foreign to a great many among the membership. Here and there, however, one can find evidence that the idea is taking root.

The Ceylon Workers Congress and its apparently successful dues collection plan, mentioned earlier, is a case in point. For a number of years the CWC, which represents some 300,000 plantation workers, was almost entirely dependent on the ample bank account of its top leader, S. Thondaman, whose father had risen from a humble background to become an estate owner of prominence. When the leadership finally decided to introduce a stamp method for collecting dues, the plan took hold—because the efforts to establish it fortunately coincided with the emergence of a feeling of labor solidarity among the plantation workers.

The background of the story was given to me by an estate manager of the region when I visited Ceylon in early 1962. The Indian Tamils, who make up the majority of the plantation workers, have always faced hostility from the dominant Sinhalese group, and for the most part have been disenfranchised. For years the working role of the individual Tamil was that of an isolated, atomized production unit. Communal solidarity within his own ethnic group was his one possible bulwark. The estate manager told me it had been interesting to watch the lateral spread of this solidarity on the plantations during the past ten years. Here, of course, was the seed ground for union organization, which in its turn gradually provided another bulwark; out of the interplay came the sense of labor solidarity that now exists. The manager admitted wryly that the increased resort to collective action had at times been hard to live with, but he felt that the whole development had been a necessary stage in the creation of a responsible work force.

It is precisely this sense of group solidarity on a working-class basis that is still missing in many of the union situations. The cultural and ethnic cleavages in the societies of most of the countries and the low level of economic development combine to work counter to the establishment of strong and steady loyalties to a trade union. Such loyalties can probably not be achieved until the labor force begins to contain a preponderance of workers whose system of values can reflect the impact of the industrialization process. Up to the present, the industrial worker has retained many of the attitudes of a nonindustrial society, and industry has as often adapted its operations to those attitudes and values as it has tried to change them. According to one observer, "the impact of foreign influences on the worker in the economy has been primarily as an element in a technology. It has not been on him as a member of a system of social values and ideals."[8] Thus at the Aramco refinery in Saudi Arabia, for example, recruitment is not from the labor force at large but restricted to particular tribal or regional groupings which have traditionally had a claim on certain skills.

[8] Thomas B. Stauffer, "The Industrial Worker," in S. N. Fisher, ed., *Social Forces in the Middle East* (Cornell University Press, 1955), p. 96.

Leadership Problems

The leadership of the organizations is a very mixed grill in terms of unions elsewhere. The leaders tend to be an elite group within their own societies, and, especially in Asia, to be "outsiders" to the industrial framework. There are, of course, exceptions. The leadership in the Malayan plantation workers' union has a manual, working-class background; however, the fluent English spoken by the secretary general, P. P. Narayanan, despite his limited formal education, marks him as unusual. He is not an "outsider," as the term is used locally, but his intelligence makes him one of the "elite." The financial secretary, H. R. Choudhury, was a plantation clerk who evidently possessed enough education to push him above the average worker.

In Asia, doctors, teachers, civil servants, and, most frequently, lawyers devote either part- or full-time to the task of trade union leadership. Especially in India and Ceylon such professional people, frequently of high caste, have assumed direct leadership. In Singapore, members of the intelligentsia operate from behind the scenes as advisers to the unions; as a rule, they are political figures, using their links with the unions to influence and guide them politically. They are outsiders, but often become extremely dedicated and capable leaders.

Mrs. Maniben Kara, president of the 40,000-member Western Railway Employees Union in India, is typical of the dedicated, social-welfare-oriented "outside" leader who has given years of service to the trade union movement. Mrs. Boze, a leader of the Calcutta dock workers union and, in 1962, elected president of INTUC, was caught up in the movement as a consequence of her work as a physician in the port. S. A. Dange, secretary general of the Communist AITUC, is a Brahman from Bombay. The rosters of many other Indian unions include officers with similar distinguished backgrounds; so far, leaders tossed up from the ranks are in the minority—and most of them were formerly clerks, who constitute a certain kind of worker aristocracy.

The Ceylon Federation of Labor has as its president Dr. N. M. Perera, a graduate of the London School of Economics, who is president also of one of the major port workers unions and the head of one of the two Trotskyite parties. The independent Ceylon Mercantile Union is led by Bala Tampoe, a well-known lawyer, who also represents—and influences—other unions. CWC's S. Thondaman, the influential estate owner, was mentioned earlier. The Government Clerical Service Union is led by a former middle-level civil servant. The Ceylonese Communist federation is headed by Peter Keuneman, an economist, who is also the leader of the local Communist party.

In Africa, clerks in private industry, middle-grade employees in government, and teachers frequently assumed the leadership of labor centers in the early stages of organization. While they are not outsiders, having actually been members or leaders of local unions, they represent a social stratum that has had relatively little direct contact with, and perhaps not much understanding of, the urban proletariat; they probably constitute the kernel of a future middle-class society. Of the more recent leaders, a good many are university trained. Others have had only a secondary education or less, but in present-day Africa even a limited education can precipitate a person into a position of responsibility. John Tettegah, secretary general of the Ghana TUC, formerly worked as a stenographer for commercial firms; Mahjoub Ben Seddik of the Moroccan UMT was a railway clerk; Abudul Al Esnag, secretary general of the Aden TUC, works full time as a white-collar employee of Aden Airways; the secretary general of the Confederation of Arab Trade Unions was a sales representative for a pharmaceutical house in Egypt; Tom Mboya, formerly leader of the Kenya federation, once worked as a sanitary inspector for the city of Nairobi. The chief officials of several other Kenya groups—among them the railway union, the Mombasa dock workers, and the general agricultural union—all appear to have had a white-collar background.

To many of the governments the "outsider" who leads a labor movement is highly suspect, and some of them have attempted to restrict the number of nonworkers who can engage in union activities. For example, Indian legislation was reportedly pending in 1962 that would prohibit outside leadership among government employee unions; in Pakistan outside leadership has been limited to 25 percent of any given union.

But to hold that the outsider is only a political opportunist is an over-simplification.[9] Many of the intellectuals working in the trade union field are motivated by a sincere regard for the labor movement.

---

[9] K. N. Vaid, lecturer at the Delhi School of Social Work, in his study of unions in the New Delhi area, comments on the number that are led by outsiders. "Almost all the effective unions are run by seven or eight individuals who are not workers. They initially organized these unions and continue to guide them." Earlier in the study, he refers to the textile unions in Delhi: "Unionism has been strong where consistent outside leadership has been available over a long period of time. This outside leadership has mainly been made available by the political parties." See Vaid, *Growth and Practice of Trade Unionism* (University of Delhi, 1962), pp. 81 and 45.

It is obvious that many others entered union activities to build a political force—but not necessarily with sinister intent. And among the leaders who stem from the earliest organizing years, a good number were probably not much aware of the political benefits to be derived until after the event. The unions, and the union leaders, often had political responsibility thrust upon them; the sharp repressive measures taken by some of the colonial powers "often forced the anti-colonial nationalist leaders either into clandestine operations or into activities politically less objectionable to the colonial administrations, such as the organization of labor."[10] Frequently, when a party was outlawed during the pre-independence period, the labor unions would fuse their political and economic functions and become more deeply committed to political operations and objectives. This was the experience, for instance, of both the Kenya KFL and the Moroccan UMT.

In any case it seems clear that the members of this educated elite, whether they are outsiders as in Asia or quasi insiders as in Africa, have fallen heir to union leadership largely because they spoke the language of the foreign colonial officer and the foreign businessman, the language in which the transactions of direct interest to the worker were, and still are, conducted. Their education also made them conversant with the modern technical and political concepts being introduced from the outside. They were an essential link between the administrator-employer group on the one side and the workers on the other, and they were needed as well to interpret events and institutions deriving from a foreign culture.

The language problem is one that the new leaders must contend with for years to come. In India, for example, out of the score of languages the only one common to both north and south is English. Gandhi, in his attempts to foster Hindi as the national language, could not be understood by the majority of his audiences in south India.[11] In Nigeria there are reportedly some 250 ethnic groups; in Ghana, among the hundred or more tribal groups, five main languages and twenty vernaculars are used. One may well ask what value the periodic union

[10] George E. Lichtblau, "The Politics of Trade Union Leadership in Southern Asia," *World Politics*, Vol. 7 (October 1954), p. 86.

[11] The INTUC for a time put out a Hindi version of its journal *The Indian Worker*, as well as an English edition. At first the Hindi edition carried full texts of resolutions and policy statements, while the English carried summary texts. Later, because it was felt necessary to communicate upwards to the many businessmen, government leaders, and bureaucrats who did not speak Hindi and because only a limited number of the membership could read in any case, this procedure was reversed. Finally, in the face of financial difficulties, the Hindi edition was scrapped; as of early 1962, *The Indian Worker* was published only in English.

meeting has, when, as in Ghana, "the multiplicity of languages habitually used by workers is so great that . . . broken English was the only means of communication possible at union meetings. It is a means of communication so crude that it is impossible to introduce any shades of meaning into it whatsoever."[12]

Top-notch labor leaders can be found in almost all of the new countries, some of them a good match for their counterparts in Europe or the United States. The problem is that there are too few of them—partly because the outstanding individual is often quickly claimed away by political and governmental operations. Seconds-in-command and able local union leaders are in even shorter supply.

The kind of staff problems that may plague the top leadership are indicated by a 1961 report of the General Agricultural Workers Union in Kenya. The secretary general of the group had been offered a training course in West Germany by the German labor movement; immediately on his departure, the union started to disintegrate. He was finally forced to abandon the opportunity and come home. In a section of the report headed "Staff Changes" are these comments (quoted verbatim):

> Since January there have been many changes of staff in Branches. Such changes occurred because of: (a) misappropriation of union funds; (b) disregard of existing Kenya laws and in particular the money collection bills which gave powers to the administrative authorities . . . to issue funds collection permits to union representatives whom they were satisfied with, in regards to their character; (c) inefficiency. . . .
>
> The unrecorded weaknesses and habits of most of our branch secretaries are: (1) some of them were too young for the post of a branch secretary—where he has to be tempted by the good amount of cash they collect from the members. . . . (2) Some of them indulged into heavy drinking, most of the expenditures in the Branches was shown as used on transport, yet money was used in the bars. (3) Due to the age of the Union and difficulty of transport in visiting the farms, most of the staff we had were of unreasonable calibre with less [limited] educational qualification.[13]

The secretary general is a soft-spoken, engaging young man with an excellent sense of organization and a reputation for personal integrity.

[12] R. B. Davison, "African Labour Studies of (1) Migrancy and (2) Industrial Relations Within a Factory in the Gold Coast" (Library of Congress; microfilm), p. 403, cited by Lester N. Trachtman, "The Labor Movement of Ghana, A Study in Political Unionism" (unpublished M.S. thesis, Cornell University, September 1960), p. 85.
[13] Secretary General Hermann A. Oduor, *Mid-year Report, 1961, General Agricultural Workers Union* (Nakuru, Kenya), pp. 9-10.

The report gives ample evidence of the difficulties he faces in building an efficient organization and training a cadre.

Certain leaders are so completely "outsiders" that their path to power is difficult to trace. Some interesting evidence is provided by a 1959 Board of Inquiry report on a Nigerian labor dispute:

> The record of the Union's activities over the years makes a most pathetic reading. . . . There have always been instances of endless strifes, distrust, intrigues, tribal discrimination, police arrests, litigation, rifts of members into factions, one faction trying at one time or the other, and often quite successfully, to overthrow the other from office, and to instal itself into power. . . . The Nigerian Union of Seamen is notorious for not appointing its officers constitutionally; it is doubtful whether the present officers were constitutionally appointed.[14]

The method by which S. O. Khayam was appointed secretary general in 1958 is then described: "He accepted his present post through the request of certain fellow students in England and some Nigerian crew whom he met at Liverpool."

Reading between the lines, one senses behind the turmoil and chaos thus detailed a political and ideological struggle among factions which has never been resolved. The secretary general was almost certainly not tapped for office in the casual way reported here. It is much more likely that he was sent in by a political faction which momentarily had enough influence to succeed in taking over the organization.

It must be noted that such factionalisms based on personal and political rivalries are rife in many of the unions. Ideological differences are responsible for much of the conflict; the split, for instance, between Mboya and Odinga within the Kanu party in Kenya, which spilled over into the trade union area, has been identified with the poles of the cold war—Mboya facing West and his rival facing East. It is not uncommon, however, for ideologies to be used by union leaders as blinds, to mask more purely personal ambitions. But whether the factionalisms result from real or feigned ideological splits, they are one of the reasons why political unionism may represent a threat to the fragile economic and political systems of new nations.

There is no dodging the evidence that a good many of the new labor movements contain somewhere in their hierarchies varying degrees of opportunism and careerism and, to a lesser extent, gangsterism and corruption, although to say that such aberrations are general would be unfair and inaccurate. A recent study of African unionism notes that

[14] Federation of Nigeria, *Report of the Board of Inquiry into the Trade Dispute Between the Elder Dempster Lines, Limited, and the Nigerian Union of Seamen* (Lagos, June 1959), pp. 4-5.

numerous organizations—especially those at the local level—suffer because their leaders are ignorant of union practices and principles; are prone to file nonexistent union registrations to serve various purposes not directly related to unions; lack negotiating skills; fail to prepare sufficiently for hearings before government bodies; tend to call strikes without consulting the membership.[15] Similar deficiencies have no doubt at one time or another afflicted new labor movements throughout the world. In the present case, the factor of conflicting ideologies makes them all the more likely—and more difficult to deal with.

White-Collar and Government Unions

In contrast to the pattern of unions of the West in their early stages, "worker solidarity" in Asia and Africa has often spread first among white-collar workers in both government and the private sector. Bank employees, for example, in India, Ceylon, Lebanon, and Morocco have developed militant organizations. The 2,500 members of the Ceylon bank employees union, an industrial type covering all workers up to the level of supervisor, were on strike when I visited the island in late January 1962. The strike was in defiance of the law, but the government did not so decree it. Earlier in January the Casablanca bank employees had begun striking one day each week, also in defiance of the government.

Throughout Africa, government employees, many of them white-collar workers and subprofessionals but with a good contingent of manual workers as well, can be said to constitute the core of trade union organization. In French West Africa in the late 1950's they made up 60 percent of the total union membership, though they represented only 30 percent of the employed labor force. Their groups were also the most efficiently organized.[16] It is also reported that government employees were the first to organize in seven African territories and among the first in six or eight others. Transport workers, more often than not those employed by government, were the first to form unions in at least ten of the African territories.[17]

[15] Nan S. Waldstein, *The Indigenous African Trade Union Movements of Nigeria, the Federation of Rhodesia and Nyasaland, French West Africa, and the Belgian Congo* (Center for International Studies, Massachusetts Institute of Technology, April 1960; hectographed draft), pp. 98-99. The list of indictments was drawn up for Nigerian unions, but it could be duplicated for a number of countries.

[16] Elliot Berg, "French West Africa," in Walter Galenson, ed., *op. cit.*, p. 206.

[17] Charles A. Orr, "Labor and Nationalism in Africa," unpublished manuscript, Roosevelt University, 1962 (hectographed), pp. 29-30.

In India, the railway unions have organized as many as 30 percent of the million employees on the state-owned system.[18] In Singapore, of the 124 registered unions, 40 represent public employees. The government workers of all categories in Ceylon are organized in two independent federations and together claim 200,000 members—an obvious exaggeration inasmuch as this figure is higher than the number of central government employees. Whatever their numbers, there is ample testimony to their influence: Ceylon's trade union act specifically prohibits federations of government employees, but no move has been made to apply the law.

The relatively steady employment by former colonial governments in both Africa and Asia of a good number of indigenous workers, whether white-collar or blue-collar, accounts in part for this high percentage of early and efficient organization. But there was undoubtedly a much more compelling reason for the early spread of worker solidarity among white-collar workers in both government and private enterprises. Since these men and women were in general literate, and some of them much better educated than most of their compatriots, they were apt to register a high fever of frustration when, day-by-day, they faced the discriminatory rules that favored the European over the African or Asian. Organization was one means to reduce their frustration; having acquired group solidarity, they later found that they were in a key position to mount pressure against foreign rule.

Rarity of Collective Contracts

Although the present basis of labor organization in nearly all of the new countries is obviously more political than economic, the "political" unions from their inception have not failed to make job-related demands and to press grievances. Strikes very frequently stem from efforts to promote the well-being of workers on the job or to protect those who have been disciplined or fired. In 1958, when the Kenya Federation of Labour started its organizing drive, there were ninety-six strikes. In 1959 the number of stoppages declined to sixty-seven, but more workers were involved, with many more man days being lost.[19] Some of the strikes were for union recognition, others for improved pay and conditions. The situation in Kenya in this respect is not essentially different from that of other countries.

[18] Charles A. Myers, "India," in Walter Galenson, ed., *op. cit.*, p. 31.
[19] Colony and Protectorate of Kenya, *Labour Department Annual Report, 1959* (Nairobi, 1960), Appendix VIII, table 10(b), p. 59.

A primary and typical demand of government employee unions in French West Africa during the post-war period involved "equalization," i.e., salary raises for the African civil servant to include all the special payments that had long been made to Europeans—housing allowances, overseas differentials, and so on. This was in part an economic issue, but it soon took on unavoidable political overtones which dwarfed the economic side.

The point to be stressed here is that the entire process of collective action by labor in these countries, even when a dispute is restricted to economic issues, very seldom takes place within a framework which can be identified as collective bargaining in a strict sense of the term; such a phrase as "collective demanding" or "collective relationships" is presently more apt. The labor contract as we know it in the West is still a rarity in these countries. Instances of its use are increasing, but sometimes with curious results. The contract between the Indian Aluminum Company and the unions in its plants, for example, almost duplicates one that might be negotiated in the United States. Yet there is something synthetic about it; the Indian personnel manager, who was trained in North America, obviously applied the tactics of his educational setting. It is therefore not a typical contract.

That so much of the area of collective bargaining has been usurped by government efforts to determine wage levels reduces the value of the signed contract at present. Wage boards in Ceylon have, for instance, handed down decisions for 24 industries or economic sectors covering approximately 800,000 workers. In Kenya, the colonial government in the early 1960's was still fixing minimum wages in nine urban areas on the advice of the Wages Advisory Board, as established by Ordinance Number 1 in 1951. Minima usually become the going pay rate.

Government intervention in the wage-setting process has been, and continues to be, characteristic of policies in the countries that were formerly British colonies, despite the announced objectives of introducing and promoting collective bargaining. What this means, of course, is that genuine collective bargaining finds difficulty in establishing roots under present economic and political conditions. As a result, labor of necessity relies largely on government action in this regard.

The use of governmental machinery to determine wage levels came under challenge in India in 1952, when V. V. Giri, a former union leader, served as Minister of Labor. Believing that spoon-feeding by the state could only retard union growth, Giri had stated his determination to move toward a system of independent bargaining. The Giri policy formed the main subject of debate at the twelfth session of the Indian

Labour Conference, October 1952, in which the Minister criticized the whole labor court system as leading to wasteful litigation and resulting in a weakening of the trade unions.[20]

By the end of 1953, Giri had lost his fight to change the basic system of industrial relations initiated during the time of British control. He withdrew his proposals "reluctantly" and resigned in 1954. Even the trade unions, including the Communist AITUC, refused to support his point of view. His successor, Khandubhai Desai, former secretary general of the Textile Labor Association and former president of the INTUC, summed up the prevailing disagreement with Giri's desire to stimulate free bargaining: "Society cannot allow workers or management to follow the law of the jungle."[21]

Given the embryonic state of unionism in these regions, it is not surprising that the collective contract embodying a wide range of conditions to regulate the conduct of management and labor is not in wide use. Neither management nor labor is yet sufficiently self-disciplined or experienced to infuse such a contract with real meaning. When one reads or is told that a "contract" is being negotiated, the word often refers to a letter of agreement or a protocol covering a single item under dispute. Such agreements are somewhat comparable to the early contracts negotiated by the new industrial unions in the United States in the 1930's, a good many of which were no more than a single sheet of paper whereby the employer recognized the union as a bargaining agent, as the National Labor Relations Act of 1935 required him to do after the union had won an election under the Act's provisions.

On the basis of the composite profile offered above, the trade unions in the developing countries appear to be feeble instruments indeed. None of the activities which are associated with strong labor organizations in the industrialized countries of the West can they carry out efficiently. Yet, as indicated in Chapter One, they also appear to be a significant and influential force in most of the new countries at an early stage of their own development, as well as of national development. How do we reconcile the conflicting evidence?

An answer to that question will be pursued in the next four chapters. Chapter Three will explore (1) the various political settings in which

[20] Morris David Morris, "Trade Unions and the State," in Richard L. Park and Irene Tinker, eds., *Leadership and Political Institutions in India* (Princeton University Press, 1959) , pp. 268-278.

[21] *Hindustan Times*, July 25, 1956, cited by Charles A. Myers, *Labor Problems in the Industrialization of India* (Harvard University Press, 1958), pp. 147, 280.

certain labor movements of the West arose, and (2) the specific setting in which these new unions arose, and which gives them, as I have contended, the character of "political unionism." Chapters Four and Five will consider the general and specific factors of "political unionism" and lead us to Chapter Six, which deals with the operating dynamics of these organizations—the techniques utilized within a fluid political situation to magnify the importance of their role.

CHAPTER THREE

The Political Setting and the Union

AN EVOLVING LABOR MOVEMENT in any country is obviously shaped in part by a multitude of factors external to itself. Among these, the political setting looms large, and a study of unions necessarily includes an examination of it. This is especially important in regard to the developing countries, where the mix of politics and unionism appears to be a potent elixir with side effects we do not fully understand.

Although there are possibly as many "settings" as there are new countries, the collective expression is used advisedly, for each mainspring of political action has had remarkable similarity to every other one, and has variously been called nationalism, self-determination, or independence. The direct involvement of trade unions in the total political process has gone hand-in-hand with the all-important efforts of political leaders to introduce the mass of workers rapidly to the politics of "independence" (which may or may not mean "freedom" as defined in the West).

In no other era has there been a situation quite like this. There is a striking contrast to what happened in the political evolution of the now developed countries of the West, where the gate of mass participation in politics was opened slowly, and only after a long period of institution-building, during which the legal, constitutional, social, and economic systems became based firmly enough to withstand whatever might be the consequence of the introduction of popular suffrage.

Political Development in the West

Before the beginning of the industrial revolution in the late eighteenth century, most of the western world conducted its politics in an atmosphere not unlike that of the exclusive clubs of the period. Political participation was reserved for small groups of aristocratic and wealthy men, and government was virtually by cliques. The pressures generated by industrialization and the consequent clamoring for recognition from formerly ignored economic groups combined to produce gradually broadening participation in the political system. As the suffrage was extended to people lower down on the economic and cultural ladder, the modern political party came into being—about 1850 in Europe, somewhat earlier in England and the United States where universal white male suffrage was granted by 1840.

The development of the political party met the need for an extension and elaboration of ties between the power groups in charge of the political machinery and the expanded electorates. The party mechanism was a means not only for bringing partisan supporters into the political process, but also for giving the leadership control over these new followers. When the electorates were limited, control and manipulation had been easy through face-to-face contacts and favors granted to the privileged few; extension of the franchise called for organization—and party platforms and ideological concepts came into play as a means of mobilizing support. With each extension of the right to vote, more of the economically depressed elements of the population were drawn into the political system, in whose name leaders could make claims for egalitarian policies. The game of politics became much more complicated as the contestants tried to absorb the wider and wider demands.

In those countries where the ruling classes were able—and willing—to effect a compromise with the new political forces that demanded greater participation in the political system and greater security within the economic system, a fair degree of consensus developed, which left the basic institutions of the society more or less intact. Thus in England and northern Europe the Anarchists, the Syndicalists, and the Revolutionary Socialists eventually became only figures in a history book. The English gentry, standing on a firm constitutional base and confident in the economic viability of the system, made the necessary accommodations, and much of the new social movement found outlet and expression in trade unionism, rather than in overt revolution. The Socialist leadership in England, probably as a consequence, was primarily reformist and gradualist in approach. In continental Europe, on the other hand, the laboring class was faced by a much more intransigent property-owning class; the revolutionary ferment therefore ran stronger, and, especially in southern Europe, has not yet dissipated itself completely.

The failure of the property-owning classes in France, Italy, and Spain to come to an understanding with the newly urbanized workers led to the virtual withdrawal of large segments of the wage-earning class from participation in the political system, destroying all hope of consensus within the society. In the 1890's the French trade unions opted for Georges Sorel's syndicalism, and much of the Spanish and Italian work force also fell under the influence of Sorel, as well as that of the Russian Anarchist Mikhail Bakunin. The "pure" trade union strain, originally dominant in the Italian labor movement, was overcome by political spokesmen whose radical programs were appealing to workers who had come to feel that they had "nothing to lose but their chains."

At the turn of the twentieth century, the worker in southern Europe, shut off from participation in the politics of his nation, economically impoverished, without education, seemingly doomed forever to a life without hope for himself or his children, readily responded to revolutionary propaganda which promised the destruction of the existing political system and the establishment of a new economic order. Later on, the Communists were the natural inheritors of the revolutionary tendencies implanted by the Anarchists and the Syndicalists.

In Italy the political system was sabotaged, not only by the Socialist left, but by the Catholic right, which boycotted the election procedures for the first forty-five years of the existence of the Italian state that was geographically unified in 1870. Thus, the politics of the parliamentary agencies were distorted and unrepresentative of the people; the consequent ruptures in the political system have persisted to the present. The social tensions building up within the lower economic ranks often found expression in the streets and "before the barricades."

In the history of all social and political change, one pattern is usually a constant: at some point the old elite must face the demands of a rising new class—must take account of what Maurice Duverger has identified as "contagion from the left."[1] If the franchise is extended at "appropriate" moments to ever-growing numbers, as it has been in the stable democracies, political movements or parties spring up to articulate the demands of the new citizens, and the egalitarian ideas are eventually and peacefully translated into legislation. This "inherent drive to the Left," as Seymour Martin Lipset has put it, may be followed by a swing to the Right, but in the meantime legal measures

[1] Duverger, *Political Parties* (Wiley, revised edition, 1959), p. xxvii.

have increased the "relative power and security of the lower strata."[2] Even right-wing dictatorships will approve the passage of advanced social legislation in their effort to win over the masses. In the more stable countries of our time the leftward drive took place relatively slowly, and moved farther in some countries than in others; in the Scandinavian countries, for example, the pace of change has gone faster and farther than in the United States (where perhaps the phrase "moderately liberal" is more accurate than "leftward"). But if the process is too long delayed, momentum is provided for the growth of revolutionary movements.

Interest Groups and Pluralism

An important factor in the development of the West's political systems has been the emergence of special-interest groups (of which the trade union is one) to serve as links, and also buffers, between the ordinary citizen and the government. The multiplicity of such groups, often with overlapping memberships, has contributed largely to the system of countervailing power that especially distinguishes modern democracies from totalitarian governments.

The interest group absorbs the raw demands of its members, collates them, sometimes adulterates them in the interests of the majority, and finally articulates them in a form whereby they may be acted upon at the appropriate place within the society. Although it may be merely a passive instrument, much more often it is creative and introduces programs and policies into the political and economic system. It plays a serviceable dual role—on the one hand, aggressively making demands on society for its members, on the other, acting as a restraining mechanism over the membership and thus helping to stabilize the political system.

That such groups do contribute to political systems is especially confirmed by situations from which they are absent or in which they lack enough influence to make their presence felt. In India, for example:

> The absence of large numbers of strong and independent organized groups in Indian politics is a major factor inhibiting the growth of parties concerned with issues of public policy rather than broad ideological questions. Interest groups, especially when they are concerned with the specifics of public policy, tend to be a bridge between professional politicians who

[2] Lipset, *Political Man* (Doubleday, 1960), p. 281.

are often forced to unite and to make compromises in order to win their support.[3]

The modern states in West Europe and North America are also characterized, in contrast to the traditional societies of the East, by a high degree of specialization in function. Executive, legislative, and judiciary branches are usually clearly defined, and the difference between the operations of the bureaucrat and those of the politician is readily distinguishable. This division of function when combined with an extensive network of voluntary special-interest groups represents a protection to the individual citizen against arbitrary decisions of the government. It must be emphasized, however, that the pluralistic society can function effectively only when the majority of its component parts are in general agreement as to the values they wish to represent and maintain. The Indian Socialist, Asoka Mehta, had this in mind when he wrote: "As much thought needs to be given to the democratic techniques of evolving political consensus as is currently being given to the techniques of economic planning, because the latter cannot succeed without the former."[4]

It is easy to forget that, if the western style of democracy does now have merit, much of what we ourselves consider worthy of emulation developed against a background of conflict. The United States experience in self-government almost foundered in its early years on some of the same weaknesses that today plague the leaders of the new countries. Separatism and exaggerated demands for states' rights denied power to the center when it was needed. And in discussing the European parliamentary democracies, there is also a tendency to forget the conditions that prompted the sweeping revolutions of 1848 and the French Commune of 1871. After all, Marxism and communism originated in Europe, as movements of protest against oppressive social and economic institutions.

It is particularly important to remember that American trade unions, which are in general now accepted rationally as a part of the normal power structure of the United States, were born into a hostile political climate (against which, in certain areas, they still must contend) because they were a new and unwanted challenge to the status quo. West European union movements also had to contend with governmental

---

[3] Myron Weiner, *Party Politics in India* (Princeton University Press, 1957), p. 264.
[4] Mehta, "The Opposition in the New States," in Edward Shils, et al., *Democracy in the New States*, Papers of a Seminar held in Rhodes, November 1959, sponsored by the Congress for Cultural Freedom (Prabhakar Padhye, New Delhi, 1959), p. 96.

and private repression of their efforts to organize. In short, labor organizations were among the last of the major power groups to win acceptance in the pluralistic societies, the sanction lagging far behind the establishment of a firm base for industry and capital.

Political Problems of the New Countries

In sharp contrast to all of the above, the developing countries have, immediately upon coming to statehood, entered the stage of politics of the mass through enfranchisement of the total adult population. Thus what Duverger saw as "contagion" when suffrages were increasingly extended in western political developments might be called "immersion" in the new countries. All classes of the society are in a position to make demands upon the political and economic system to an extent never experienced in the West at such an early stage of development. Because many of the political systems are relatively weak or brittle and are not yet fully structured, the governments have great difficulty in absorbing the innumerable problems with which they are faced.

The first elections in India after independence illustrated how rudely the so-called equilibrium of a political system can be shaken when the ballot is suddenly extended to greatly increased numbers. The long-established political dominance of the Brahmans was abruptly challenged in several states when the more numerous members of lower-caste groups sought a place in the sun. The long-term effect may well be beneficial, but in the short run such a radical change increases the difficulty of forming a cohesive nation.

The prior political experience of many of the government and party leaders has in general been limited to creating a one-dimensional instrument designed to win independence—typically, the "movement" front or Congress, encompassing such ill-assorted bedfellows as religious sect adherents, wealthy landowners, Socialists, Communists, bankers, Boy Scouts, and trade unionists. Once independence was achieved, the instrument often proved poorly designed to rule a country.

In India, for example, where industrial development had proceeded to the point of separating social and economic classes and providing a background for ideological and special-interest schisms, independence brought an almost immediate rupture of the Congress Party. Its leaders determined that Communist domination of the labor unions could not be tolerated and set out to establish their own union federation, the Indian National Trade Union Congress (INTUC). This move, plus others, forced the Socialists who had operated within the Congress Party to establish a separate party and a union federation, the Hind Mazdoor Sabha (HMS). Again, Morocco's nationalist party—the Istiqlal—fell apart three years after independence, with the union wing splitting off from the more conservative elements of the old liberation front.

In most of the countries, however, every effort has been made to prevent a breakup of the liberation movement and to maintain the momentum built up during the pre-independence period. In some of the newly independent African states, where the political movement devolves on one party, the effort tends to suppress opposition. Relevant to the present existence of the one-party systems is the fact that the bulk of the population is still largely undifferentiated into social or economic levels. Thus there is justifiable doubt that such unitary political instruments can continue to exist once economic development has taken hold and the separation of classes begins. In any case, the involvement of the masses remains just as important in post-independence days as it was before.

Under the new circumstances, the drive to elicit mass participation in the political processes—and hence support—is part of the drive toward national integration. Ideology, usually of the nationalist variety, is still an important technique in winning mass support. The leaders of the new countries are almost forced to define the legitimacy of their rule in terms of the people themselves. When the regime becomes the embodiment of the people's aspirations, the leaders can play upon the sense of frustration and the ill-defined, but nevertheless real, pressures for change which exist in the society. "Thus modern nationalism has much more social revolutionary ideological content than nationalism in 19th-century Europe. . . . This new nationalism involved a growing preoccupation with the changing pattern of economic and social development and a desire to promote it."[5]

The politics of independence is the politics of change. Associated with a sudden break with the past, it often takes on a radical coloration, as William L. Holland, writing on Asian nationalism, points out:

> It is worth noting that in all the countries . . . there is a widespread but ill-defined acceptance of socialist or near-socialist ideas in economic and

[5] *Ideology and Foreign Affairs*, U.S. Foreign Policy Study No. 10, prepared for the Senate Foreign Relations Committee by the Harvard University Center for International Affairs (January 1960), p. 37.

social policy. There has been a far reaching permeation of Marxist and Communist, as well as socialist, concepts and clichés. These have become an essential part of the intellectual equipment of not merely the intelligentsia but also the political leaders, and curiously enough, many business men.[6]

The same observation can be applied to Africa, where in many cases the leaders "have borrowed from Leninism the concept of 'democratic centralism' and of the state party as a revolutionary vanguard. . . . The adaptation of Communist ideas and methods has been in some cases very extensive."[7] Even in Egypt officials talk about "the real revolution" to come, and President Nasser on occasion resembles a student of Lenin when he precedes the word "capitalist" with "corrupt" or "exploitive."[8]

Most of the governments throughout Africa, the Middle East, and Asia describe themselves as socialist. What precisely they mean by this is not clear, but at least it is evident, on the one hand, that they fall short of communism and, on the other, that western social democracy has little appeal at present to the new leaders. A government may be most reactionary in regard to civil and political rights yet maintain a left-wing economic policy—the classic free capitalism model being rejected out of hand. (This is not surprising, since a distorted version of the model was part of the hated colonial picture.) It is clear enough, however, that most of the states have reached out eagerly for the so-called advanced economic doctrine associated with state socialism. These are regimes that were "born in revolutionary struggle and . . . once in being they strive to maintain revolutionary momentum. The movement to displace the pre-existing system of order then becomes a revolutionary movement for national renovation, or a movement to carry the revolution beyond the national borders, or both."[9]

The general identification of the new countries with leftist economic programs is attributable to a number of factors (some of which will be more fully discussed later). One of the factors is certainly related to the aforementioned need of the governments to enlist the support of the masses for a dynamic forward thrust; another is the increasing number of people who are actually participating in the political sys-

[6] Holland, ed., *Asian Nationalism and the West* (Macmillan, 1953), p. 7.

[7] Walter Z. Laqueur, "Communism and Nationalism in Tropical Africa," *Foreign Affairs*, Vol. 39 (July 1961), p. 615.

[8] As he did, for example, in a taped television broadcast for Columbia Broadcasting System, Aug. 24, 1961.

[9] Robert C. Tucker, "Towards a Comparative Politics of Movement-Regimes," *American Political Science Review*, Vol. 55 (June 1961), p. 283.

tem and consequently are in a position to make demands on the economic system.

The level of political participation of individuals in countries which are 70 to 80 percent rural and oriented toward the value system of a traditional society is difficult to estimate. Sometimes it can be seen that government and party leaders use their mass following only as a manipulated sounding board for ideas. If the manipulation produces a specific reaction, this provides justification for the next step to be taken. However, the percentage of an electorate that actually casts ballots, even under a manipulative situation, affords some insight into the extent of popular participation in the affairs of a nation.

In India's first national election, held in late 1951 and early 1952, 103,000,000 people, 45 percent of the electorate, voted; in 1957 the figure was 49 percent, in 1962, 56 percent. In Morocco, the first elections were held in May 1960, for the purpose of setting up municipal councils. There were 47,000 candidates in 10,000 districts; 74 percent of the registered voters cast ballots.[10] In Kenya, in the spring of 1961, 884,000 or 84 percent of the electorate took part in the elections for the legislative council.

Among other signs of participation are the following. In the Italian UN trusteeship of Somalia, twenty political parties had developed before independence. Political expression from the French Cameroun was registered in 1956 to the extent of 35,000 communications sent to that year's spring session of the UN Trusteeship Council on a matter concerning the Cameroun area.

A recent study of the 1961 elections in Kenya provides an interesting illustration of the political awareness of rural voters, whom it is customary to regard as wedded to old patterns of life and cut off, sometimes willfully, from sources of ideas and information.[11] Approximately 260 farmers and rural leaders were interviewed in the election district of Central Nyanza to determine what they knew about the seven candidates running from the district. The responses showed an awareness certainly as high as would be found in many a town in the United States—and possibly higher. Some 83 percent could give the name of the man who turned out to be the winning candidate, and 75 percent could identify the runner-up. A high percentage could link a candidate with his party. When the interviewees were asked to assess the types of

[10] Douglas Ashford, "Elections in Morocco: Progress or Confusion?" *Middle East Journal*, Vol. 15 (Winter 1961), pp. 7-9.
[11] George Bennett and Carl G. Rosberg, *The Kenyatta Election: Kenya 1960-1961* (Oxford University Press, 1961), pp. 160-163.

political or social problems which demanded attention from the legislative council, 18 percent said that increased educational opportunities
were most needed; 12 percent ranked problems related to land use as
of paramount importance. Other issues cited included taxation, unemployment, opportunities for business, all phases of national development, and, of course, the campaign for independence.

The political structuring of the new countries is taking place at the
same time that political education is commencing for vast numbers of
the population and during a period when radical elements in the society have the greatest opportunity for seizing control. The difficulties
normally expected or anticipated in forming a new nation-state are
aggravated enormously because of the need to compress the time factor
in the solution of complex social, political, and economic problems.
The new leadership must run fast and achieve, or seem to achieve,
miracles—for this was their promise, their campaign platform when
they involved the masses in the campaign for national independence.
Their justification for remaining in office is directly related to visible
evidence of progress.

Because populations are growing at high rates, the time element in
the development equation is of great significance to all who are trying
to build politically viable states and to those who are supplying development aid. India and Egypt are caught in a two-way squeeze: when
their development process started, surplus population was already in
being; as of 1960, India's rate of growth was 2.2 percent per year,
Egypt's 2.4 percent. In Pakistan the 1961 census revealed a population
at least 6 million greater than had been projected on the basis of
previous figures. Ghana estimates of growth run from 1.4 percent to
as high as 3 percent. Even such countries as Syria and Iraq, which at
present have land room to spare, foresee a large percentage of their
economic progress negated by the present rate of population growth.

The imperatives placed on the leadership of the developing countries
and on the suppliers of foreign aid are great. Failure to progress can
only lead to an erosion of the position of the governments in power,
which in turn creates tremendous pressures to turn away from the use
of democratic methods. To impose solutions by authoritarian means
can seem to be an easy and quick way out of the vexing problems
faced by the new governments, whereas democratic institutions take
time to develop and mature. The unitary party systems which, with
some few exceptions, are associated with the new African states, can

easily become instruments of suppression. The suppliers of foreign aid need to know much more about these systems than is known at present.

Even in India the opposition elements among the multiple parties circulate in clusters around the Congress Party, and no one of them represents a truly national opposition. The problem of developing a national consciousness in all of these new states involves the conflict between the traditionalists and the modernizers—a conflict that provides a rationale for moving toward suppression of opposition. Edward Shils, in discussing the papers presented at the 1959 Rhodes conference sponsored by the Congress for Cultural Freedom, asked:

> Was it an accident . . . that much of the discussion of parties did not refer to the problems of political parties in the new states? So many [of the conferees] went down the path of digressions so eagerly, or so willingly—because they could not find a place in their affections for political parties, and because they had no more than a lukewarm belief in the value of parties. I came away with the impression that with the exception of Masani and Mehta, there was a general sense that parties are often not "real," that they too often are the vehicles of small cliques or narrow sectional interests, and parliamentary life lacks inherent persuasiveness and authority.[12]

This theme was reinforced by another of the participants, Albert Hourani:

> . . . modern political thought in the Near East, and I suppose elsewhere, has been thought about the question of how to generate a common will. This explains why at one period, those who wanted national independence also wanted parliamentary institutions; the example of Europe, they thought, showed that representative government was the means of generating this active will. But it was only a means, and might be replaced by a better means. In the new states of the Near East the fundamental conflict of politics is not that of democracy against dictatorship. Indeed for most people this conflict does not raise a question of principle at all. There is not real contradiction between the two: they are both means to the same ends of national dynamism, and the only question is which is the better means.[13]

A western visitor to the developing countries is told by many spokesmen that civil liberties are not nearly so much on the minds of men as he would have supposed, and that the twin concepts of economic development and national independence are much more evocative of

[12] Shils, "Old Societies, New States," in *Democracy in the New States*, pp. 14-15 (see footnote 4, above).

[13] Hourani, "The Regulative Principle of Society," in Shils, *op. cit.*, pp. 158-159.

action. There is, of course, a big "if" here: are the spokesmen accurately representing the people at large? One can, however, find plenty of evidence that awareness of the importance of individual liberty is not pronounced in Asia or Africa.

For example, I had occasion in 1962 to ask an influential member of the Ghana Convention People's Party what "democratic centralism"— a phrase much in vogue in the country—meant to him. He seemed to appreciate that a westerner might well be puzzled and concerned about the phrase, and said, "This would be much easier to explain if we were not speaking in English. The concept is not foreign or new to those of us associated with tribalism. In my tribe we have always had the system of paramount chiefs and subordinate chiefs, and the word of the paramount chief was final. The subordinate chief who would not accept the dictate of the paramount chief, once the decision had been made, was eliminated from office." He may have been quite accurate when he implied that the system was popularly acceptable. Yet it seems unfortunate that a party dedicated to modernizing the society would, even to reinforce its power, so readily adopt a traditional value system described by a phrase that brings to mind the most ruthless system of political control in modern history.

An American commentator on democracy in Africa has pointed out that even though an independent state may use governing methods which westerners would not consider liberal it is not therefore "totalitarian":

> The citizens do not live in terror of a secret police. Political debate is a commonplace of African life. Opposition to government policy exists, is heard, is even listened to. Policies change; the composition of governments changes. There is an enormous amount of give and take in almost every independent African state.[14]

He concludes that the present form of political organization is a necessary step toward a more liberal system. The conclusion seems highly debatable, although I recognize its theoretical validity. The subject will be considered again in later chapters.

[14] Immanuel Wallerstein, *Africa: The Politics of Independence* (Vintage Books, 1961), p. 159.

The Place of the Trade Unions
in the Political Setting

The unions in the developing countries must accommodate to the political framework and to the ideological web within which the framework functions. They are particularly in the grip of nationalism, which, more than any other single factor, influences the policies of the union leaders. However, a prototype model of a union is hard to find, because the political patterns through which nationalism is implemented from state to state display divergencies, and these are reflected in the labor movements. Ghana and Senegal both have, to all intents and purposes, one-party systems. Yet Ghana's system is marked by aggressiveness and intolerance toward criticism; in Senegal the tone is softer, even permissive. The respective trade union situations reflect this shade of difference: e.g., multiple unionism is permitted in Senegal. The political systems of India and Ceylon are "open"—and union competition is rife.

Despite the divergent political patterns, all of the new regimes face certain common problems: the need to create political consensus and to integrate separatist elements; the drive for economic development; the incipient radicalism; and the imperative demand for quick solutions. The unions are directly involved in the process of seeking solutions. In some countries—e.g., Ghana, Guinea, and Kenya—the unions have influenced the development of political institutions. In others—e.g., Egypt, Liberia, and, insofar as INTUC is concerned, India —they have fitted into the niche assigned to them by political superiors, but are by no means devoid of influence. Even in the countries where fragmentation of the political forces blurs the picture, it can still be seen that union development, as elsewhere, has in the main been shaped by the pattern of political events.

It is essential that this point be understood by the westerners who are encouraging unionism. If the political groupings consolidate into a one-party structure within which there is a high degree of unity, the trade unions are also consolidated. If the political groupings are highly fragmented—often as a result of religious or ethnic or ideological divisions in the society being transferred onto the political stage—so too will be the labor groups. Occasionally a labor movement takes the lead in setting a pattern, as the UMT did in Morocco in 1959, when its break with Istiqlal forced the party to establish a new labor arm. (Relatively unimportant, the new federation has nevertheless been a thorn in the side of UMT.) Generally, however, the political winds are strong enough to dominate the labor organizations and in large measure determine the path they will follow.

That this may be true even before a party takes over control of a state, and thereby gains access to the coercive powers of the executive and legislative machinery, was clearly demonstrated during the vote of the French West African territories in 1959 on continued association with France. The labor organizations all belonged to the regional Union Générale des Travailleurs d'Afrique Noire (UGTAN), the trade union wing of the Rassemblement Démocratique Africain (RDA), the political association. In each of the territories the unions tried to produce a "no" vote, although the individual parties in all of the countries concerned (except Guinea) were in favor of continued association with France. The union effort failed completely, even in the cities. Guinea was the only country to opt out, and this was because Sékou Touré, as both political leader and trade union leader, was able to dominate the scene. It must be noted, however, that UGTAN influence was on the wane before this event, possibly because the political ideas the component unions articulated ran counter to those of the political leaders in the individual territories.

In general it is evident that while the unions are highly political under certain conditions (discussed in Chapter Four), they have not as a rule dominated political developments, even when, as in Guinea and Ghana, they had been one of the more influential core groups in building the victorious political force. A typical post-independence party, developed from the liberation movement, continues to maintain its specialized subordinate units in the trade unions, as well as in students' associations, women's organizations, and the like, although in most cases some degree of limitation is at this stage placed on the operations of the groups. Control of the trade unions can be subtle and light, as in the open political system of India; almost complete, as in Egypt where union leaders have very little voice; or strong but appreciably less than total, as in Ghana where the unions have a considerable amount of power within the one-party regime. In each case, however, unions associated with the party in power are expected to march in step with the national goals established by the party.

After independence, a labor movement, whether it is part of the regime in power or in opposition to the government, inevitably loses

some of its former influence and may even be looked upon with suspicion by the government, whose aims must now broaden from the
scope of the pre-independence struggle. The free-wheeling strikes and
agitation of the earlier days are not now in the national interest, and
labor leaders are asked, or ordered, to redefine the role of the trade
union in the society. Emphasis is likely to be placed, not on assuaging
the discontents of the worker, but on devising methods of disciplining
and controlling the work force as a productive whole. When a union is
in opposition to the government—e.g., the AITUC in India, the UMT
in Morocco, and the Trotskyite union in Ceylon—it can play a more
traditional role for the workers, limited, however, by legal restrictions
and bureaucratic pressures.

Whatever the political picture, the unions and their leaders exert a
surprising amount of influence. This is not, however, a reflection of
absolute power. Rather, it is an indication that the labor movements
are among the very few interest-group centers of power that have
organizational structure (even if loose and rudimentary), leadership,
and a direct sense of purpose that usually runs counter to the traditional and sometimes obstructive elements in the polity. Since the
larger associational interest-group structure to which we ascribe such
great value in modern societies has not yet evolved in most of these
countries, power has been thrown into the hands of the labor groups.
Under such circumstances the union leaders have become spokesmen,
not only for their own small membership, but for the entire urban
labor force. In some instances their influence spreads even more widely
—to all of the city population, and some of the rural.

Finally, it is important to point out what may be the most essential
difference between union development in the new countries and that
in Europe and North America. The labor movements in Africa and
Asia, like those in many western countries, were at one time subject
to government repression and opposition, but the governments in this
case were not African or Asian. While it is true that official British
policy—and French policy in later years—encouraged the establishment
of unions in the colonies, the divergent objectives of the native unions,
which even at an early date were politically motivated, and of the
colonial administrators inevitably brought on conflict.[15]

On the other hand, these unions have been part and parcel of the
movement that brought (or is bringing) the indigenous political forces
to power. The record of hostility and suspicion that pertained in the

[15] The policies of the colonial governments are discussed in Chapter Five.

West when labor movements first began to disturb the serenity of intrenched capital does not exist here. Therefore, though there may be differences of opinion or even open ruptures, the union leadership is not basically at odds with the new governments or with the political structures behind them. This has permitted the establishment of party-union and government-union relationships of a type quite unknown to many western labor movements—especially to those in the United States —which have affected not only the nature of unionism, but in certain instances the nature of the emerging political structures.

CHAPTER FOUR

Political Unionism

TRADE UNION FEDERATIONS in the developing countries, with very few exceptions, are active and direct participants in the evolvement of the political systems described in the preceding chapter. They are seeking, have found, or have had imposed upon them a political partner. The end product of such affiliations may be strong or weak, depending on the specific circumstances of the political force or movement of which the unions are in some degree a component part. Even in the Middle East, where in most instances government restraints prevent overt party-union connections, the labor movements are highly political.

As stated earlier, it is the thesis of this book that the "political unionism" which at present typifies labor organizations in Asia and Africa is a product of the milieu in which they operate. Some of the factors that account for the characteristic were briefly defined in Chapter One; here they will be discussed in more detail, along with other background elements of the political picture as they affect the unions. Again, however, it must be emphasized that although the characteristic is dominant, it is not exclusive. Further, in suggesting that nearly all organized labor activity in the new countries is dominated by one given trait, I am not disregarding the numerous national variations. But when a cross-check is made from country to country in both Africa and Asia, certain traits can be observed that are common to unions in many of the countries. I conclude, therefore, that such traits stem from similarities in the background "radiation" to which the labor movements have been exposed. It is these background similarities that are highlighted here, because they are important to an understanding of the whole process of political modernization in an evolving nation, and to the union role within the process.

Western analysis of the union role has to a large extent abstained from making the cross-check that reveals these similarities. Instead, it has attempted to equate the new unions in time and stage of evolution with established labor organizations in the developed countries; thus it persistently relates to the simple theory that labor movements are a reaction to capitalistic industrialism and will therefore develop along a course wherein political drive is secondary to economic drive, and indirectly accomplished. But capitalistic industrialism is not yet a commanding force in the new countries, whereas the relevance of political viability to economic development is highly manifest—and the political drive of the labor federations can be seen on every hand. In a very broad sense, the drive is related to the present rapidity of economic and political change in these areas, which in turn is producing great pressure for general social change.

This statement obviously needs to be refined, since one can also say that the United States, over the past fifty years, has experienced rapid change and that American unions became basically more "political" during that period. On the whole, however, the changes tended to reinforce the unions' use of indirect methods to achieve ends that must be engineered through political means. Various brief flirtations with direct political affiliation have usually been abandoned when union leaders recognized that the price, in terms of the main union function, was too high. Paying it would have meant going into the wilderness of complete isolation from the main stream of American thought. In other words, U.S. labor organizations had a choice throughout the period of change, and the result was a certain adaptation of their earlier role to fit more modern political ends—but they were not overwhelmed by political necessity, for it was always possible and relatively safe to go along with the gradually "paced" extension of social rights. The unions in the new countries at present have little choice: the change is radical, an abrupt departure from previous norms, and up to now its nature has been primarily political.

Political Fluidity

One of the most important background factors is the correlation between political unionism and the stage of development of a given political system. In all of the developing nations a period of ferment is part of the process of gaining independence and establishing a new political entity. During the colonial period, widely disparate elements could and did unite politically for the purpose of driving out the foreigner. After independence, a struggle usually emerges between the indigenous forces still clinging to tradition and separatism and those dedicated to political and economic modernization. At the same time, within the camp of the modernizers there may be an ideological struggle involving both ends and means. There is, for instance, the three-pronged issue of capitalism versus a mixed economy versus socialism. There is also the question of whether solutions can best be reached through democratic or authoritarian methods. Such struggles are bitter, and the unions are usually deeply and directly in the middle of them.

This battle of ideas is being conducted within political structures which in many instances are as underdeveloped as the economies. There are discontinuities or weaknesses in the political institutions, glaring defects in the supporting bureaucracies, imperfectly formed party structures, scarcities of leadership at all levels, gaps—vertically and horizontally—in the means of communication, and a damaging lack of intermediate bodies and interest groups to help sort out manageable segments of the people now directly involved in the transition from one type of society to another. Given such conditions—which in combination frequently resemble a political vacuum—it is understandable that the unions are drawn into the political process and that political leaders try to buttress their positions through trade union support. The labor leaders in the main provide a counterweight to forces in the society which seek to organize power around traditional religious, caste, tribal, or linguistic groups. Because the general thrust of trade union effort is toward modernization, it is a valuable adjunct to the modernists who are trying to build new social, political, and economic structures.

The weaknesses in the political structure are put under further strain by the economic and political demands from the vast numbers of the newly enfranchised. The system has thrust citizenship on the masses in most of these countries (other than in the Middle East), and the new citizens are invoking their rights by making claims upon the system. But these people are largely still under-represented in and before the existing parliamentary institutions, and also have few of the channels that in the West are provided by special-interest groups through which to express themselves.

In this situation, the labor organizations have been in a strategic position to articulate the demands, not only of their own membership, but also of people who lacked other advocates. Political and labor leaders alike were quick to see the usefulness of the unions as political carrying agents and as reservoirs of massed power that could be manipulated to political advantage, especially during the period of opposition to the foreign government in power. "Where political parties remained only loosely organized and leaders remained dependent upon a cluster of semi-independent groups for their support, the art of political survival depended heavily upon the skill in maneuvering and manipulating a congeries of distinguishable interest groups. This gave the articulate spokesmen of particular interests a prominence in political affairs they might not have otherwise had."[1]

Lack of Requisites for Economic Unionism

Much of the push that turns the new labor organizations in the direction of political unionism derives from the continuing lack of an industrial base. This means, first of all, that there are relatively few targets for collective bargaining. Government is still the biggest employer. In most of the African countries, for instance, government workers may account for as much as 50 percent of those employed and, out of the total population, roughly 4 to 15 percent is in paid employment, as contrasted to over 40 percent in the developed countries.

A 1959 survey in Kenya revealed that approximately 24,000 organizations or individuals were classified as employers. Of these, however, 50 percent employed only domestic servants; only 118, or less than 1 percent, employed 500 or more people.[2] The government, a few foreign firms, and the plantations provide the bulk of paid employment that would normally come within the sphere of organizing efforts. The average employer hires only a handful of people in addition to members of his immediate family. Obviously, cohesive organizations devoted to collective bargaining in the usual sense would be difficult to effect when there is such a lack of employers with whom to strike a bargain.

But in nearly all of the countries an even more basic factor tilts the union function away from collective bargaining. A militant, job-protective type of unionism can be practiced successfully only in an economy that is both firmly based and expanding; "economic unionism"

[1] W. Howard Wriggins, *Ceylon: Dilemmas of a New Nation* (Princeton University Press, 1960), p. 159.
[2] Colony and Protectorate of Kenya, *Labour Department Annual Report, 1959* (Nairobi, 1960), p. 40, Appendix I, Table 1(i).

is also more practicable in countries which have a large internal market or a protected external market. The economies of the new states have as yet neither a firm base nor protected markets. In countries faced by repeated balance-of-payments problems labor organizations are under pressure from employers and from government to set wages which will protect the export potential. (The balance-of-payments events of 1962 in the United States, a country which until recently had been free of concern over export markets, bear out this point.)

Some sixty years ago, Werner Sombart identified the acceptance of trade unionism and social protection legislation by business interests in England between 1850 and 1890 as related to the "coincidence of a number of circumstances favourable to capital that produced this businesslike organization of the working man." The cited "circumstances" included the remarkable growth of business, expansion of the export trade by seven times in forty years, and the increase of shipping tonnage in British harbors by sixty-five times over a like period.[3]

In the United States, trade unions developed into stable organizations only after the industrial revolution was a hundred years old and a substantial capital stock had been accumulated. Here too economic trade unionism developed from a "coincidence of . . . circumstances favourable to capitalism," which could absorb the demands of the small, organized work force for economic improvements. The major break-through in labor organization growth in the 1930's was in part an accompaniment of the political change of that period, but the change was not so radical as to divert the major thrust of union activity from the primary goal of collective bargaining.

As of the early 1960's, the prerequisites of economic unionism were almost nonexistent in most of the developing countries. Current development efforts were being concentrated on attaining the so-called take-off point from whence further development would become a self-sustaining process. Possibly India and a very few others could be assumed to be within striking distance of this magic marker. Otherwise, almost without exception, local markets for goods were restricted and countries were dependent upon the export of raw materials to finance their development. The situation does not necessarily preclude efforts to bargain for higher wages and better working conditions, and the unions do engage in such activity. But the low state of economic development unquestionably generates restraints that may push the

[3] Sombart, *Socialism and the Social Movement in the 19th Century*, translated by Anson P. Atterbury (Putnam, 1898), pp. 64, 69.

unions even more into seeking political solutions to economic problems.

All of the governments impose restraints to some degree on the
collective bargaining aspect of trade union activity. With very few exceptions, the right to organize is usually granted—and often espoused
as a method of building and maintaining a mass political base. But the
right to strike may be limited and there may be direct governmental
interference in the establishment of wage levels.

The Labor Market and Union Function

The status of the labor market in the developing countries must
be interpreted as a politico-economic factor closely tied to the unions'
assessment of their function.[4] The work force is largely made up of
unskilled illiterate laborers. Skilled workers are a very small proportion of the whole, and, especially in Africa and the Middle East, many
of them are foreigners—Europeans and South Asians—who heretofore
sometimes used their special position to block entry of local workers
into better-paying jobs. Agricultural workers compose 70 to 80 percent
of the force, and among them are a large number of migrants who
float between rural and urban employment. In French West Africa, in
the late 1950's, it was said that nearly all the 140,000 agricultural wage
earners were probably migrants, and in the non-agricultural labor force
of some 310,000 in the towns, a good many were only temporary
workers.[5]

Descriptions of the labor market are often conflicting, as the following two statements from a report of the Nigerian Labour Department
demonstrate. One paragraph reflects the seasonal labor shortages that
have plagued Africa: "Fluctuations in the availability of underground
workers in the coal mining industry cause considerable losses of output
during the farming season. Many of the miners continue to regard
mining as a part-time occupation and spend as much as one-third of
the working week on their private small-holdings during this season."

[4] I am indebted to Mrs. Clare Belman, my research assistant, for first calling this
relationship to my attention. Professor Adolph Sturmthal of the University of
Illinois noted the factor in a presentation to the April 1962 conference at the Inter-
American University of Puerto Rico, the theme of which was "The Political Role
of Labor in Developing Countries."

[5] Elliot Berg, "French West Africa," in Walter Galenson, ed., Labor and Economic Development (Wiley, 1959), p. 199.

Two paragraphs later this comment is found: "In general, there was more labour available than could be absorbed by existing industries. About five thousand candidates contested for fifty vacancies in the Nigerian Coal Corporation whilst three or four times the numbers required applied for work at the Nkalagu Cement Works."[6]

In all of the countries the coming of independence and the changes thus generated in the social scene have given new political significance to the large numbers of unemployed and underemployed. In India, for instance, the 1960 estimate of involuntarily unemployed was about 9 million.[7] Each year 2 million more people enter the potential labor force, but there is scant hope that economic development can absorb this increment for many years to come. Unemployment rates in some of the major cities are 20 to 30 percent. The situation is fairly typical of that found in the other countries.

Underemployment in agriculture adds to the total burden by pushing many people off the land to end up as unskilled job-seekers in the burgeoning cities. The case of Egypt is the most dramatic: between 1907 and 1954 the number of people engaged in agriculture almost doubled, while the crop area increased by only one fifth. The underemployment implicit in such a reduction in per capita land available, even without an improvement in methods, is staggering.

Obviously, union organization is hampered in such a labor market. Small economic units and illiterate, unskilled, and migrant workers do not add up to the creation of unified, stable memberships. When a majority of the jobs available can be rapidly filled at any time by unskilled labor, union bargaining power is proportionately reduced.

But the very factor that deprives the worker of status and bargaining power as an employee gives him great worth in the political market place. Unskilled workers, organized in general and industrial-type unions and dependent upon literate, often outside, leadership, can quite easily be attracted to direct political action. On the other hand, skilled workers, organized in craft unions, are in a strategic position to exert economic pressure on employers; once having won an advantageous position in the economy they are likely to confine their interests more closely to "bread-and-butter" unionism.

Many of the unskilled in Africa and Asia on leaving their villages

[6] Eastern Region, Nigeria, *Department of Labour Annual Report, 1957-58* (Enugu, 1958), p. 3.
[7] John P. Lewis, *Quiet Crisis in India: Economic Development and American Policy* (Brookings Institution, 1962), p. 84.

to join the urban labor force have cut some or all of their ties with the rural forms of "social insurance" that the extended family system provides. The loss of this security makes them receptive to political appeals and, usually, susceptible to political manipulation. The job and pay framework within which the urban worker functions is only one of the influences that contributes to his susceptibility. The over-crowded cities—with inadequate transport facilities, housing shortages, poor sanitation, understaffed police forces, and sometimes breakdowns in the food distribution network—make their impact. All around him he finds squalor, disease, crime, alcoholism, prostitution, and inhuman competition in the job market.

These social ills can no longer be blamed on colonial governments; the remedy for them is now the responsibility of the nationalists in power. The labor leaders, faced with this circumstance and its impli-cations, have by and large adapted the function of unionism to the present necessities. The economic power that usually accrues to a stable labor force in a stable industrial setting is for the time being not possible here, and therefore emphasis has been placed on building a political force organized around a tenuous economic rationale.

Social Imbalance

An important contributing cause of political unionism is the imbal-ance that in general typified the social systems of most of these states in their recent past. The political component of a system was often widely repressive, or used as an instrument to favor one group against the others. The economic component was almost always geared to promote the interests of a very small group, to the disadvantage of the majority, and economic opportunities for this majority were severely limited. Social stratification was rigid, access to education rare, and justice, more often than not, tailored to the amount of property owned or the color of a man's skin. When a nation emerges into political self-determination from such circumstances, it is to be expected that the primary move of its organized groups will be toward a complete over-haul of the system, and that sweeping political solutions for all prob-lems will be sought.

The unions' membership is the segment of society most affected by the previous—and in many cases still present—social imbalance. Es-pecially for the urban worker there were terrible frustrations in the environment, and the repression of the political system whenever he tried individually or collectively to better his lot has not been forgotten. In many of the countries he even lacked the language tool with which to express protest, because the holders of power spoke another tongue. (As noted earlier, the problem of upward communication is still serious, and explains in part the role of "outsiders" as leaders of many of the unions.)

One disturbing example of social injustice that recently came to my attention is related to the language problem. In 1957 a literacy program was begun in Kenya—where adult illiteracy was estimated at some 80 percent—by agreement between the U.S. International Cooperation Administration and the Kenya government. The program apparently operated most successfully, and at its peak more than 15,000 people were enrolled. In 1961, however, the program was reported to be in trouble; the Kenya government termed it too difficult to administer and asked for its withdrawal.[8] According to later information, the program was distasteful to certain groups of white settlers, who wanted the Africans to work, not read "seditious literature."

Given such provocation, it is easy to understand why demands for political change become part of the testament of dynamic elements in a population seeking self-improvement. Social distortion can manifest itself subtly and in a hundred different ways, but when it is present, the economic and social classes it oppresses can eventually be expected to react sharply, and hence to support leaders who promise sweeping change.

To recapitulate, the receptivity of the present Asian or African worker to the political approach is an amalgam of his sense of social alienation—a continuing reaction to the lack of social justice in the recent past—and the practical, and sometimes radical, manipulative operations of union and political leaders to which he is open because of his emotional rejection of the past. Partially uprooted from traditional social controls, he has not adapted completely to the more impersonal disciplines of urban living, and his experiences in the new milieu frequently introduce a high element of tension and frustration into his formerly stable family and group relationships. His perspective of the society as a whole and his political awareness are limited—but he seems to be very willing to have them augmented by articulate union spokesmen and other political leaders. In this, he is not too different from his European counterpart of an earlier era.

[8] *New York Times,* Nov. 19, 1961.

It is apparent that many workers, whether on their own or under the influence of the union leaders, have concluded that the vast array of unsolved problems which affect the social system cannot be handled through the traditional trade union approach. One analyst, in considering the marked tendency for political ideas to dominate the labor scene and take precedence over more precise trade union gospel, defines the situation thus:

> Unions cannot by themselves remove all the causes of labor unrest in the developing areas. They cannot bring about industrialization, agricultural reorganizations, national self-determination, and land and tax reforms, nor eliminate city slums, nor improve communities. Since these issues cause labor unrest and are uppermost in the minds of union leaders the emphasis placed on political action instead of collective bargaining is understandable. Indeed, if these problems are not resolved it will be difficult for traditional unionism to function.[9]

The unions play a swing role in the process by which the frustrations and fears of individual workers become dynamic when linked to the goals of individual political leaders or, as is more often the case, of a mass political movement. Under such circumstances, the advocates of "pure" trade unionism in an underdeveloped economy are usually overwhelmed by the more articulate advocates of political reformation.

The place of the articulate, educated (or partly educated) "elite" who have in general assumed labor leadership is clear. Most of them have acquired some sense of history and can therefore synthesize and translate the broad world of ideas into concepts understandable to a largely illiterate rank and file. It can be said that the situation demanded leaders who are capable of articulating protest to take on the responsibility of representing the voiceless mass. It would, however, be inaccurate to regard them as initiators of political unionism. Rather, they have helped to give drive and direction to the irresistible move toward nationalism, and after independence have continued to supply content to the movement for national renovation.

All of the new countries exemplify in some degree the conditions which produce "political unionism." They are all experiencing rapid change; their political systems are underdeveloped; economic development is still at a low level. All of them have inherited social systems

---

[9] William H. Knowles, "Industrial Conflict and the Unions," in Wilbert E. Moore and Arnold S. Feldman, eds., *Labor Commitment and Social Change in Developing Areas* (Social Science Research Council, 1960), p. 306.

containing distortions and imbalances—a high residue of social injustice. However, it must be said that not all of these conditions are needed to push labor organizations into political unionism.

In France and Italy, for example, the trade unions are to a large extent politically oriented, yet these countries are of course industrialized and have a developed political system. Only two of the several characteristics discussed above are operative here: in both countries, a highly stratified social system has been maintained and the political system has adjusted too slowly to the advent of the new industrial class, so that urban workers have long felt alienated from the rest of the society. For Italy, the impact of the industrial revolution was especially delayed.

The same can probably be said for present-day Japan, where, despite the high level of industrialization and a firm political system, most of the work force does not identify with the political system, which is largely in the hands of a financial aristocracy. Rising living standards for workers in both Japan and Italy might possibly temper the political—and generally left-wing—drive of the workers and make them less vulnerable to radical ideas, but only if the rise brings about redress of other social inequalities.

In the new countries, however, rising standards of living could not in themselves bring about a change in the other factors that at present make for political unionism. The trade unions for the most part seem to feel a great necessity to identify with a revolutionary process demanding both economic and social reformation. In this identification, they are part of the political ferment and mass groping for political equality, global in scope, which has marked the twentieth century. Because of this accident of timing, labor organizations have played a greater role in the formation of the new states than could have been predicted from the experience of unions in Europe and the United States.

The key position occupied by the new unions is, then, a derivative of certain characteristics in the political processes of the developing countries, first in the experience of winning independence, and then in regard to the problems to be solved for the future. The nature of the union function unavoidably changes with the advent of independence, whereupon new stresses are placed on the relationships formerly pertaining between the unions and the political parties. Nevertheless, under the new circumstances the unions have an important role to sustain, which for some time to come will be only indirectly related to the labor-management function.

CHAPTER FIVE

Nationalism and National Development

SINCE THE MID 1950's nationalism has been the most important overt symbol and ideological force in the political world—more powerful even than communism as a propellant of action, as the Communists themselves have acknowledged by adapting a good many of their programs and objectives to the cause of nationalism throughout the Middle East, Africa, and Asia. Always vague in its outlines and defying exact definition, this ideology has nevertheless provided the dynamic whereby a large number of dependent states, whose populations add up to a whole of untold millions, have moved to the status of independence. Often it is the only unifying force in nations created before internal consensus has been achieved on the most basic factors related to the establishment of a nation-state.

After independence is an accomplished fact, the tone of the new nations is further influenced by an outgrowth of nationalism—the drive for national development, which in a sense becomes an ideology in its own right. The fervor of the earlier drive is still present but must now be turned in a new direction, which usually means that a whole new set of rules for action must be learned.

The effect of these two specific conceptual influences on the trade union function has been direct and enveloping. Nationalism brought about labor's identification with political movements; the drive for development calls for continued political direction of trade union effort by exerting pressures that are not usually characteristic of the labor picture in the more developed countries.[1]

[1] The "mix" of political, economic, and social factors in the new countries, however, makes it extremely useful for the labor observer to know the Italian labor-political situation before visiting Ceylon or India. One author has gone so far as to term Italy the "exemplar" for those seeking greater understanding of unionism in the developing countries. See Maurice F. Neufeld, "The Inevitability of Political Unionism in Underdeveloped Countries: Italy the Exemplar," *Industrial and Labor Relations Review*, Vol. 13 (April 1960), pp. 363-386.

Although trade unions existed in some African and Asian countries before the drive for independence began to reach its fever point, it was the force of nationalism that propelled them out of their position of relative unimportance. It was the force that gave rise to new unions, and endowed both new and old with the degree of influence they have on the total social scene—a much greater degree than labor organizations in Europe or the United States had at any comparable period of their development. In a number of cases the new unions were established before new industries were anything but a token and, even more frequently, before there was a labor force cohesive enough to be recognized as such. It is evident that certain factors of expediency, external to unionism, have had a great deal to do with the birth of labor movements in these areas both at present and in the past; a digression to consider some of the factors will be useful.

Unionism As a Product of External Factors

In Africa, the first unions were formed in the 1880's by Europeans, who simply applied practices learned in their home countries. These earliest organizations and their successors were in great part concerned with protecting the privileged position of white workers against African competition. For example, the contracts between the white unions in the copper belt of Northern Rhodesia and the copper companies provided a bar to the skill upgrading of African employees until 1955, at which time the combined pressure of the African mineworkers union and one of the copper companies finally broke through the resistance of the union composed of Europeans. Twenty-four categories of jobs were then opened to African entry.[2] Wherever there was a European settler population, such resistance was typical, and it is still a major problem in Southern Rhodesia, the Republic of South Africa, and the Portuguese colonies.

During the early period the native Africans, in their efforts to adjust to this new and imposed economic tool, tried to adopt the organizing methods of the dominant Europeans, but made little progress in a setting that was essentially pre-industrial. Prior to World War II, therefore, the African organizations were small and unstable, often coming into existence for the period of a single dispute, then breaking apart—perhaps to form again under different auspices and conditions.

[2] Harold K. Hochschild, "Labor Relations in Northern Rhodesia," *Annals of the American Academy of Political and Social Science*, Vol. 306 (July 1956), pp. 43-49.

In both Africa and Asia the first impetus to union growth beyond the early rudimentary form was provided by the colonial authorities. The Colonial Development Act passed by the British Parliament in 1929, at which time Lord Passfield (Sidney Webb) was Colonial Secretary, included a provision that fair labor conditions must exist in a colony if it were to be eligible for funds under the Act. In September 1930, Passfield sent a dispatch to all colonial governors informing them that the government looked with favor on the formation of trade unions; in the next few years most of the territories passed appropriate laws.[3]

In 1938, the office of labor adviser was added to the Colonial Office and a social services department was established. Labor officers were sent into the field to supervise labor-management activities and assist the formation of unions. The British Trades Union Congress (TUC) loaned experienced people to the Colonial Office, participated in overseas trade union missions, and invited labor leaders to England for training. The 1940 Colonial Development Act was more specific than the 1929 Act: it stated that territorial governments, to be eligible for development funds, must provide reasonable facilities for the establishment and activities of labor unions.

A 1937 decree of the Popular Front Government in France gave the go-ahead signal to labor organization in the French colonies, but relatively little was accomplished before the outbreak of World War II, at which point union activity was halted. The few trade unions that were established during this early effort still bear the mark of their respective colonial sponsors structurally and operationally. The French unions which operated in Africa were affiliated directly with labor federations in France; the doctrinal imprint of the Communist-dominated French Confédération Générale du Travail (CGT) is still noticeable in Africa today.

Both the British and the French directed their efforts at establishing organizations of the collective-bargaining type. The 1952 French Labor Code for the Overseas Territories limited the purpose of unions strictly to "the promotion and protection of economic, industrial, commercial, and agricultural interests."[4] The British approach has been summed up by G. D. H. Cole in a way that reveals its underlying inconsistency:

[3] B. C. Roberts, "Trade Unions in Colonial Dependencies," *British Affairs,* Vol. 4 (March 1960), pp. 12-15.

[4] International Labour Organization, *African Labour Survey* (Geneva; 1958), p. 228.

They [the unions] were in most cases closely connected with political movements, but had an economic basis in the low standards of living and in the conditions of mining and plantation economies in backward areas. . . . The policy of the British government was to recognize colonial trade unionism and to endeavour to guide it as far as possible into nonpolitical channels.[5]

The British authorities were never successful in carrying out the second phase of the policy. But the extent of union development must be termed phenomenal, when one considers that the traditional factor which usually influences union growth—i.e., an industrial setting—was in general lacking. In 1960 there were reported to be 1,250 trade unions with well over a million members throughout the territories that were British dependencies of that time. This is the more remarkable because only 5 million people were classified as wage earners in a total population of 75 million.[6]

The former French territories have somewhat the same history of rapid union growth against the background of economic underdevelopment. In 1959, official statistics showed that there were 500 local unions in French West Africa, with a total membership of 166,000, or over 35 percent of the wage force. Harvard economist Elliot Berg has preferred to use a much lower, unofficial figure of 70,000, but even this is a substantial number under the circumstances.[7] Union growth in Morocco and Tunisia also demonstrates the sharp upward trend.

Clearly, there was a stimulus to union growth unrelated to the industrial climate. We do know that the stewardship concept of colonial administration demanded action in the social field. However, most of the colonial encouragement of union organization as one means of attacking the serious social problems overlooked an essential fact: the political and economic situation in the colonies did not lend itself to the transfer of institutional and legal practices incorporated in labor-management relations in the home countries. The indigenous labor leaders in the colonies adopted the form—but sooner or later turned the purposes of trade unionism into something quite different from those of the original model.

Lord Passfield's insight on the matter led him to recommend compulsory registration of unions. And in one of his 1930 dispatches this

---

[5] Cole, "Trade Unions: Colonial Trade Unionism," in *Encyclopaedia Britannica* (1958 edition), Vol. 22, p. 384.

[6] Roberts, *op. cit.*, p. 12.

[7] Berg, "French West Africa," in Walter Galenson, ed., *Labor and Economic Development* (Wiley, 1959), p. 206.

comment is found: "I recognize that there is a danger that, without sympathetic supervision and guidance, organizations of labourers without experience of combination for a social or economic purpose may fall under the domination of disaffected persons, by whom their activities may be diverted to improper and mischievous ends."[8] His perspicacity has been demonstrated by the events of recent years, although the nationalists would not, of course, agree that their objectives were "improper and mischievous."

It can be said that the British registration requirements and the subsequent restrictions designed to limit the unions to being instruments for collective bargaining were in essence political acts. Thus, the very steps that were taken to prevent labor from going down the political path actually provided an additional and challenging motivation for political unionism.

As originally fostered by both the British and the French, the move toward unionism was in large part a response to increasing urbanization. Anticipating future events in industrial and other economic development, the colonial powers undoubtedly recognized the serious social problems that would be posed when great numbers of people flocked to the cities to enter cash employment for the first time and were, on one hand, unrepresented and, on the other, under no disciplining agent. Local administrations would be especially concerned about the difficulties of assimilation, since at that time government was the main employer.

Urbanization has continued to be one of the factors in the birth and spread of labor movements. The problems foreseen in the 1930's have multiplied, for the increase in urban populations has outdistanced the anticipations. The growth rate of nearly all of the major cities has been especially high over the period since 1948. In Kenya, for example, from 1948 to 1960, Nairobi's population increased from 119,000 to 261,000, and Mombasa experienced an 80 percent increase.

One further external influence on the course of union development and the role the leaders have chosen to play emanated from educational institutions in England and France. Graduates of the London School of Economics, for instance, are myriad in South Asia. Many of them learned their economics and formed their political philosophies under Harold Laski and his famous colleagues. The majority became Socialists, and a good number of these saw unions as part of the ma-

---

[8] Dispatch of September 17, 1930; see Walter Bowen, *Colonial Trade Unions* (Research Series No. 167; Fabian Publications, 1954), p. 4.

chinery through which political power could be captured. The story was much the same for those who studied at the French universities and are now nationalist leaders in the former French colonies in Africa; however, they brought back with them an even more pronounced Marxist (often Communist) ideology.

Nationalism and Union Growth

Under whatever sponsorship unionism originated in these countries, the greatest aid to its growth was the spread of nationalism. Political leaders needed mass organizations for the struggles, and were therefore obliged to encourage those that existed or to create new ones. Most of the unions acquired additional influence in the society and gained supporters in direct proportion to their involvement in the liberation movements. The smallness of the labor movement in Uganda as late as 1960—in which year it included only one third of 1 percent of the labor force—has been laid to the fact that the country had not up to that time had a strong nationalist movement.[9]

Union centers have had value to the liberation movements both externally and internally. The Algerian federation (UGTA) was established primarily to open up lines of communication with international labor organizations and to keep the propaganda of the rebels before the world through speeches before the International Confederation of Trade Unions and its affiliates. Delegates from UGTA were welcomed to AFL-CIO conventions in the United States at a time when official channels of communication were squeezed tight. The federation also maintained ties with Soviet bloc unions, and has received financial and other aid from the Save Algeria Committee sponsored by the Communist World Federation of Trade Unions. The Moroccan federation (UMT) has also received substantial material assistance through its international union connections.

Inside a country, the unions had value as agents for mobilizing the strategic urban segment of the population—heightening its political consciousness and channeling the discontents of workers newly released from rural life patterns. In some cases the politics of the city were carried into the rural areas through union members whose ties with their village families were still strong.

During the struggle for independence, the unions showed their

[9] Walter Elkan, *Migrants and Proletarians* (Oxford University Press, 1960), p. 65.

muscles in political strikes and mass demonstrations—and, even when defeated, were not as a rule destroyed. The special-interest base provided a core which could be built upon (and to this extent a union was usually a more valuable asset than, for example, a student organization which, once it had staged its demonstration, often had no continuing function). Labor leaders attempted with some success to show that wage drives, solidarity strikes, and so on were related to the larger problems facing the entire native population in the struggle against the colonial powers. They could also enlist support from other elements of the population by linking the broad claims of the liberation movement with the more specific problems faced by the workers.

At least partially carried along in the liberation currents were the Marxists, revolutionary and reform alike, who saw in the situation a number of opportunities to gain control over the masses. Not at all deterred by the lack of industrial development, these pragmatists set about organizing unions designed to mobilize the masses and channel their grievances into a bid for political power.

In short, under the influence of nationalism or some other ideology, the main emphasis was placed on incorporating the fledgling labor groups, whether they came into being more or less spontaneously or were organized by "outsiders" from the top down, into broad-front political movements. Thus for the labor leaders the traditional union function was in part incidental to the main objective of building a political force. Nevertheless, they invoked the economic function as a method of membership recruitment and of winning the loyalty of members and sympathizers; they also addressed themselves to collective bargaining—or more accurately, to collective demanding and sometimes collective "begging." All of this was frequently aimed at strengthening their hands in the political battle.

Beyond this, in some cases, there was another but not often stated purpose for union activity. Oscar A. Ornati points out that unionism in India is "primarily a labor movement dedicated to the establishment of a new society. . . . With rare exceptions, Indian trade unions do not accept the society surrounding them. They are engaged in a major effort to change it. In the past, change meant getting rid of the English; now it means bringing about a Socialist state."[10] The statement could apply to all but a few of the unions in the new countries; in fact, the characteristic it describes is even more discernible in states whose

[10] Ornati, "Problems of Indian Trade Unionism," *Annals of the American Academy of Political and Social Science*, Vol. 310 (March 1957), p. 156.

political constellation is less clouded than India's. An Indian writer puts it this way:

> A purely "bread and butter unionism," which implies that the unions should be concerned only with the job-interests of their members, besides being impracticable in the underdeveloped countries is full of dangerous possibilities as well. Trade unions in all countries arose as a protest against the existing social inequalities, exploitation of man by man and attempts to deprive workers of their inalienable right to enjoy status and dignity as human beings. Thus essentially [the union] is, in one of its most important aspects, an instrument of social change.[11]

There is no doubt that during the infancy of the union movement in these countries the area of protest encompassed the entire spectrum of political and social needs and was never limited to specific industry-oriented problems. Thus the union partnership with political parties was an inevitable and on the whole triumphant part of the drive for nationalism. But when, at the time of liberation, the union role shifts to that of collaborator with the new government, the former relationship faces a great challenge and the labor movement is sometimes hard put to define its new role. The problem is spelled out in the following comment, which, though it concerns India, has general application: "The labor movement as a whole has not yet developed an attitude and an organization to help it fulfill its often inchoate aspirations. Indian labor unions have not found a *raison d'être* commensurable to that lost with the achievement of independence."[12]

Nevertheless, the links formed with political forces during the pre-independence period are important in shaping the role that unions assume later. The "nation-building" or "national-purpose" unionism which is an outgrowth of nationalism is still crucial to the drive for national development that must take the center of the stage when independence is achieved. This new drive in its turn exerts a further influence on the labor movement.

The issue of trade union relationships with governments and political parties will be dealt with in more detail at a later point. It suffices here to indicate the changing nature, as noted in the paragraph above, of the relationship for those unions cooperating with the governments in power. It should also be noted that, for Communist and other opposition labor movements, determination of role after independence

[11] Subratesh Ghosh, *Trade Unionism in the Underdeveloped Countries* (Calcutta: Bookland Private, 1960), p. 341.
[12] Oscar A. Ornati, "Indian Trade Unions Since Independence," *Far Eastern Survey*, Vol. 23 (August 1954), p. 120.

is far easier than for the cooperating unions. The opposition groups can continue as before—blending economic and political objectives in a way that will keep a government in power on the defensive.

National Development

In the press for rapid national development that is the almost immediate sequel to the installation of a liberation government, the leaders of the union federations are usually the most ardent champions of the goals espoused by the new regime. If the pace lags, they are also among the most vocal in demanding a speed-up. Because they know that both the social change they wish to promote and the success of unionism depend on economic growth, their commitment to development almost equals that of the government leaders. Nevertheless, at this stage of the partnership, conflict often arises, sometimes related to the means of achieving the mutually desired goals, sometimes reflecting personal power struggles.

Situations in the one-party states of Africa have been especially revealing in this regard. In general, the political leaders see themselves as warring against disease, poverty, illiteracy—in short, against all the factors that spell backwardness. During the crisis period they concede no room to the factionalism that stems from opposition parties. The attitude has a superficial logic; inasmuch as they also contend that there is no division of economic classes in their nations, there might appear to be no need for parties to represent various segments of the population.

But the trade unions come very close to providing such special representation. Therefore the labor leaders are confronted by an ambivalence: they must try to satisfy the claims of the union membership without transgressing the claims of their political partnership. If they ignore the wage demands of the membership, they may risk losing their power base. On the other hand, government and party pressures for resistance of such demands, until development plans are more firmly in process, are strong—and the punishment for disregarding the pressures can be swiftly administered.

It is possible, even probable, that some African unions may contemplate jumping the partnership traces as their membership gains stature and confidence and asks more pressingly for special benefits. Even though labor supports the general goals of the government, the question of how much development versus how much consumption may loom large. Agreement on both sides that rapid development is necessary does not preclude conflicting interpretations of the specifics involved.

Another point of tension is the not too remote possibility that a union center might become the party's political rival, or that union leaders might threaten to replace present political leaders. In Ghana, for example, the secretary general of the Trade Union Congress, John Tettegah, is considered in some quarters to be a competitor to President Nkrumah. Tettegah could be easily removed under the present circumstances, but such a step would not be taken lightly by the government, since his utility as the operating head of probably the most fully developed interest group in the country is considerable. In Tanganyika, when Prime Minister Julius Nyerere resigned in February 1962 to take over full-time leadership of the Tanganyika African National Union (TANU), there was speculation that certain sections of the trade union movement contained the seeds of a political opposition which had threatened his control. Whether this was true is not so important as the fact that the speculation existed. In any case, the possibility of the threat was circumvented by a shake-up in the government and the appointment of C. S. K. Trumbo as High Commissioner to London. As president of the important railway union, Trumbo had shown signs of being disgruntled and having an opposition movement in mind.

The Union's Nation-Building Role

Despite such party-union conflicts in Africa and elsewhere, the communality of nationalism, national development, and the trade unions is illustrated by the shift of a number of labor leaders to positions of political and governmental influence in the period immediately preceding independence and thereafter. Although this also reflects (1) the scarcity of leaders skilled in the use of political techniques, (2) the drive for power of some of the labor leaders, and (3) the fact that the unions provide a base from which this drive can be launched, it testifies most of all to the fundamental identification of the trade unions with the total political structure. Conflicts notwithstanding, government in these countries is not an enemy aligned with business interests to thwart the unions, as government once was in Europe and the

United States; it is an amalgam of the forces that brought it into existence.

A number of the governments have made it clear that the trade unions have specific political functions to perform—some of them domestic, some in the foreign policy field. According to the Ghana government, the Ghana TUC has another purpose to serve besides that of "protecting and advancing the interests of employees in relation to employers." Much more important is "its political purpose as the wage-earners' wing of the Convention People's Party. Mr. Tettegah has often described the relationship of the TUC and the CPP as that of Siamese twins and Ministers have been equally anxious to identify their party with the TUC."[13] (There has been some evidence, however, that certain groups among the workers have begun to regard the TUC as a substitute for the CPP; this is what gave rise to the rumor of Tettegah's competition with Nkrumah.)

Not all of the countries assign unions a similarly active role in the nation-building process; in some cases the labor leaders are expected to play their party-supporting roles solely by soft-pedaling their demands for worker benefits, and in all other respects to be passive. In many more cases, however, union leaders themselves consider it a part of their active responsibility to the developing state to tailor the economic demands of their membership to national goals.

P. P. Narayanan, who directs the Malayan plantation workers union, which is essentially non-political, exemplified this viewpoint when he remarked in a recent speech that unions had "to play a role in creating a climate conducive to the attraction of foreign capital in their lands within limits and with necessary safeguards. They may, perhaps, refrain from volatile and irresponsible expression likely to have adverse effect on foreign investors and making them shy to invest."[14] Although the majority of union leaders are far more overtly dedicated to the attainment of political objectives than Narayanan is—and not so concerned with the welfare of the foreign investor—most of them are just as deeply committed to national development and thus can be depended on to serve as a moderating influence in the formulation of union economic demands.

[13] Douglas Rimmer, "The New Industrial Relations in Ghana," *Industrial and Labor Relations Review,* Vol. 14 (January 1961), p. 216.

[14] Speech to the Educational Institutions and International Labor Conference, Kellogg Center, Michigan State University, March 25-30, 1962.

Exceptions to the foregoing definition of the nation-building role are of course provided by unions that stand in opposition to the new governments and by those in countries such as Pakistan, where ideology has at present little significance. The opposition organizations, whether Communist or not, are limited only by the requirement (usually understood rather than stated) that they play—at least ostensibly—the part of a "loyal opposition" and continue to support the nationalist concept. The Moroccan UMT, for example, is able to represent its membership aggressively and even militantly. It has, however, also been engaged in building the usual "movement-type" structure, composed of a political affiliate, youth groups, a woman's organization, and so on. If the political-labor movement in Morocco should eventually come into political power, there seems little doubt that the UMT would then conform to the general pattern wherein unions become an integral part of the governing complex.

Restraints on Collective Bargaining

The collective bargaining function of all the unions in the new countries has been affected and limited by government restraints. The development plans adopted by most of the governments give at least lip service to economic planning, which usually includes some attempt to fix upon a national wage policy—a delicate and difficult undertaking even in the most highly developed society. The "policy" that results is often nothing more than a poorly thought-out edict to the effect that wage increases are untenable because they are inflationary. Most of the governments, authoritarian and democratic alike, have instituted some form of compulsory adjudication of labor disputes and even cases having to do with individual grievances are frequently handled by a government labor court of some kind.

Union leaders in general have acquiesced in the establishment of these arbitration procedures for two reasons: first, this was a way of substituting political power for the economic power that most unions still lack; second, most of the labor leaders subscribe to and support the idea of a planned economy, and they are not, at least for the time being, likely to protest any manifestation of such a plan, even if it may spell future difficulties. One difficulty has already cast its shadow: as squeezes in the economy occur, the judgments handed down by the

governmental adjudicators and policy-framers become more conservative. In Ghana, for example, the 20 percent wage increase granted
by decree in 1960 was effectively wiped out in 1961 by a compulsory
tax and savings plan instituted by the Nkrumah government.

In the early days of independence, the wage board system did indeed
pay off for the work forces, whether in Indonesia, India, or Africa but,
as noted above, it may not do so now. Morris David Morris claims that,
dating from 1934, state intervention in India has been the basic means
by which the social product was distributed, and consequently the
union function was to maintain discipline in the work force. He concludes, therefore, that the development of Indian trade unions took a
direction which places them closer to the Soviet model than the American model, and will probably continue in that direction.[15] Morris over-
states the case, I believe, in his association of the Indian system with
the Soviet model, but he does identify a factor that is common to most
of the new countries, namely, that the determination of wage levels is
in large measure a government function.

Despite the restraints, collective action directed at winning benefits
or security through more or less normal negotiating techniques is not
at all unusual. As noted earlier, the railway unions in Africa, which
were the first organizations to achieve some degree of cohesion, were
doubly useful to nationalist causes because their effectiveness in carrying out job-related representation of their membership created political loyalty. The federation of general agricultural workers in Kenya
has negotiated a detailed written agreement, which, among other
things, calls for a check-off of dues. The dock workers union in the
port of Mombasa has developed, through negotiations as well as government intervention, an extensive web of rules providing increased
security and income to the port worker. The rules include a check-off,
shift differentials, vacation benefits, and even the decasualizing of a
large portion of the port labor force.

According to an interesting study of trade union activity in the
British Cameroons, the Cameroons Development Corporation Workers
Union had apparently been collecting dues consistently for some years
from a high percentage of its members and performing "the functions
of a modern trade union quite effectively, within the limits imposed

[15] Morris, "Trade Unions and the State," in Richard L. Park and Irene Tinker,
eds., *Leadership and Political Institutions in India* (University of Princeton Press,
1959), p. 270.

by the lack of experience of its leaders. It has carried on its negotiations responsibly and fairly effectively, so far as the opportunity has been open to it to do so; it is in touch with the needs of its members and works for them continuously in individual matters; it has done much to regularize and advance relations between employers and work-people and to improve working conditions."[16]

The Aden Trade Union Congress, although devoted to the furtherance of nationalist goals, has, over the period of the last six years, nevertheless carried on the collective-bargaining function fairly effectively. It has developed a high degree of cohesion, engaged in strikes lasting as long as ten weeks against a major European oil refinery, and developed a system of dues collection which makes the union independent of outside financing.

A story told of a little-known strike at Luanshya in Northern Rhodesia illustrates the unconventional bargaining techniques sometimes employed. "After a strike vote had been taken, some 10,000 workers and their families, totaling perhaps 30,000 persons, overnight left the mine compounds and camped quietly in the bush for three weeks, until their demands were conceded."[17]

These examples of more traditional union activity illustrate once again that there is more than one facet to the operations of the Asian and African unions, and that in the choice of approaches open to the labor leaders, the collective bargaining or demanding route is not ignored. As noted earlier, the "demanding" function is frequently a tactic to gain political support, but there are numerous occasions when a union employs collective action for no other purposes than those stated in its list of demands.

The spread of collective bargaining has not been encouraged by management, the third part of the industrial relations triangle. Some employers have resisted the process with all the power at their disposal; others, who were not essentially against it, resisted because they were unskilled (as many of the early union leaders were) in its intricacies. Only very recently in several of the African countries have employers begun to band together to work out constructive policies in regard to

[16] W. A. Warmington, *A West African Trade Union* (Oxford University Press, 1960), pp. 127-128. I have not been able to ascertain whether the consistency of dues collection has continued beyond the date of Warmington's study.

[17] Melville J. Herskovits, "The Organization of Work," in Wilbert E. Moore and Arnold S. Feldman, eds., *Labor Commitment and Social Change in Developing Areas* (Social Science Research Council, 1960), p. 132.

relations with the union representatives of their employees.

Generally speaking, the specialized conditions which mark an under-developed economy will probably militate for some time to come against the development of collective bargaining in the American sense of the term. There is considerable tugging and hauling which can loosely be described as the initial stages of a collective relationship, and this can be expected to grow in importance if the economies them-selves develop according to the plans. For the present, the unions are generally willing, and frequently able, to carry on direct bargaining with employers—if for no other reason than to develop in the member-ship a sense of loyalty that can be transformed into political currency.

Multiple Unionism and Collective Bargaining

In the countries that permit competing parties—among them India, Ceylon, Singapore, and Indonesia—political unionism is usually also multiple unionism. The ability of an organization to carry on collec-tive bargaining is reduced by multiple unionism because it frequently prevents the building of a unified policy for dealing with employers. When a number of unions are involved in a competitive struggle, usually carried on at the plant level, attempts to arrive at clearly de-fined bargaining procedures are frustrated. To establish the principle of exclusive representation to facilitate orderly collective bargaining is of little use so long as political currents circulate through the work force; if one union is excluded from the plant in terms of economic representation, political cells would certainly be established by the "outs" to compete unofficially with the "ins."

Some of the power thus lost at the bargaining table is made up for through pressures which can be applied against the political structure. This is particularly true when one of the competing political forces uncovers an issue around which it can build unity of action from below that will lead to strikes and mass demonstrations. The govern-ments which exercise a large amount of control over the trade union field through legislation, etc., are forced to react to any challenge to their authority; demonstrations and strikes therefore invariably ac-quire political connotations, no matter what specific dispute generated the original union action. This facet of union operations will be treated in more detail in Chapter Six.

Most of the factors discussed in the preceding pages are operating to some degree in nearly every one of the emerging countries of Africa and Asia. Generated by the interworking of the co-concepts nationalism and the drive for national development, they provide the rationale for the determination of trade union function and role. Thus it has come about that, with only a few exceptions, the labor movements have placed emphasis on integrating the unions with a broad-based political movement.

The economic bargaining function of the unions is circumscribed by the basic commitment to nationalism and to economic and social development under state auspices in a setting of scarce physical and human resources. Most of the labor leaders accept this in theory and, with some modification, in practice. There is nothing illogical or unnatural about the choice they have made; they are responding to clear signals which point the direction to be taken.

CHAPTER SIX

Dynamics and Techniques

THE READER IS NOW ASKED to recall that the concluding section of Chapter Two commented as follows on the composite profile with which the chapter was mainly concerned: "On the basis of the composite profile . . . , the trade unions in the developing countries appear to be feeble instruments indeed. . . . Yet, as indicated in Chapter One, they also appear to be a significant and influential force in most of the new countries at an early stage of their own development, as well as of national development." The question was then asked, "How do we reconcile the conflicting evidence?" The three succeeding chapters pursued an answer by exploring past and present backgrounds, environmental factors, and ideological concepts that have affected the character of the unions. This brings us to the point of examining "the operating dynamics of these organizations—the techniques utilized within a fluid political situation to magnify the importance of their role."

It should be apparent by this time that "trade unionism" is a singularly inaccurate term to describe the activities of these groups—unless the whole framework within which they function is considered. And in using the term, it is important to understand an essential difference between the organizing base of the new unions and that of unions in the United States, which in turn relates to the difference in objectives and functions.

American trade unions are "exclusive" organizations. A new member must pay an initiation fee, and thereafter must pay dues. If, over a certain length of time, his dues are not paid, he is expelled, and this often means loss of employment. The leadership of a union expends a great deal of effort to protect the "purity" of the organization by fencing it off from the encroachments of "outsiders"—which term is applied widely, even to members of other unions. The major thrust is to protect the jobs of men and women who occupy a given position at a given time. This is in accordance with the classic description of trade unionism as enunciated by Commons and Perlman. The exclusive nature and job-oriented thrust of the American labor movement is reinforced by its structure, wherein local unions are affiliated with national or, in labor parlance, international organizations, each of which fights continually to maintain its autonomy and to establish watertight compartments marked "exclusive jurisdiction." The net result is a highly tenuous relationship among the hundred-odd national organizations and between each of them and the presumed parent, the AFL-CIO.

In contrast, the unions in Africa and Asia are "mass" organizations. Far from being exclusive, they embrace all who will show active interest in their propaganda message, and usually even those who may be only lightly or sporadically touched by it. In other words, they conceive it to be their function to stir the masses and indoctrinate them with the spirit of change. Thus, the union voice is projected to bring members, non-members, and even non-workers to the support of union and party objectives.

The Mass Labor Organization

The concept of a mass organization has been conspicuously missing from the American scene since the demise of the Industrial Workers of the World. The following definition of the concept concerns the IWW and was written in the mid 1920's (at which time the IWW was actually expiring), but it applies surprisingly well to the function of the unions in the new countries.

> Achievements of propaganda organizations cannot be gauged by membership. . . . The secret of success for a propaganda organization is a select group of individuals with initiative, intelligence, and militancy. Such organizations must bring together a group of evangelists who can inspire and proselytize—in short, what the IWW terms a "militant minority." Propaganda organizations are primarily interested in cultivating ideas and sentiments and, if at all successful, extend their influence far beyond the narrow bounds of membership.[1]

The types of worker with which the IWW in its heyday scored its greatest successes—migrants and newly arrived foreigners, often illiterate, who were not yet an integral part of American society—roughly equate with those courted by the unions in the developing countries.

---

[1] David Saposs, *Left-Wing Unionism* (International Publishers, 1926), p. 165.

However, the IWW differed from these present mass organizations in that it failed (almost perversely, it seemed) to build lasting groups, being content to hit and run. Its chances of success as a revolutionary instrument were limited from the beginning by the United States' unique social, political, and economic setting, yet its significance to the American scene was far greater than a modern researcher would assume if he consulted only its limited membership figures and the sometimes bizarre record of its leaders and their actions.

The movement-conscious labor leaders in Africa and Asia are looking "far beyond the narrow bounds" of the constituency typically embraced by the trade union, although their organizations are built around a core of traditional economic unionism. In essence, the functions of these unions are as frequently scaled to propaganda objectives as they are to economic objectives. Under the circumstances, the holding of periodic membership meetings to discuss matters of immediate relevance to the workers has no particular value. But much pulling and hauling at present goes on between management and labor, and a good deal of steam is applied to "collective demanding." A large part of this, however, is actually designed to win increased political support. In the countries that permit party competition, perhaps at least 50 percent of the jockeying for position among various unions represented in a given plant situation is related to each group's hope of increasing its political influence among the workers. And as we have seen, the union leaders, and consequently the unions, usually relate political influence to an ideology. The ideology may be nationalism, communism, socialism, or—among the government-sponsored unions of South Asia—anti-communism. Even those leaders whose connection with unionism began as no more than a bald grab for political power frequently later become ideology oriented.

There are, to be sure, a number of unions (for example, those in Pakistan, Iran, Lebanon, Turkey, and some states in Southeast Asia) which are not identified with a movement or much versed in the use of mass organization, either because they lack a binding ideological concept, or are severely limited by government controls, or possibly have not achieved operating maturity. In such cases, as noted earlier, the union function is tied to a series of *ad hoc* maneuvers that attempt to strengthen the position of the organization and the influence of individual leaders. Unionism of this type is still political. Its goals are simply short-range and limited—and sometimes fearfully corrupt.

But the more noticeable pattern in both Asia and Africa is the virtual partnership between political party (and/or government) and the union, with the party providing the political objectives and the union working to mobilize the masses.[2] The differentiation is not always as neat as that, for the political leader may also be the union leader; Dr. N. M. Perrera, head of one of the Trotskyite parties in Ceylon and also president of the Ceylon Federation of Labor, is a case in point. And a former union leader may become an important party official, as Tom Mboya of Kenya has. In fact, one of the interesting features of the mergers which are characteristic of political unionism is the way the roles of the players often defy ready identification. It is a little like trying to locate the pea in the old shell game.

Ample evidence is nevertheless to be found that there are "rank-and-file" leaders in all of the unions who devote the main part of their time to activities normally associated with labor organizations. They maintain contact with the workers, conduct gate meetings, enroll new members, and carry out numerous administrative chores. But also woven into the pattern are nearly always a number of threads that lead eventually to a political figure or a party. The union leader usually needs political support and the political leader needs a mass base. The function most expected of the union is that of providing a channel of communication between the political elite—which may be the government in power or a party in opposition—and the masses. In the best situations the channel is two-way.

The Unions as Links

To be effective in this channeling function, a union must have the widest possible mass character, and it must have means for mobilizing its indoctrinated membership or sympathizers for action on command. It is claimed by Robert C. Tucker that the organizational forms used by these "movement-regimes" are direct offshoots of Leninist principles of organization.[3] Certainly there is some relationship between

---

[2] K. N. Vaid identifies three types of political-labor relationships in his study of unionism in the Delhi area, stating that the differences are of degree, not of kind: "dependent" unions, which are completely dominated by the political parties; "sphere of influence" unions, which are semi-independent but lean heavily on political parties for guidance on important matters; and "independent" unions, which maintain close relationships with parties. See Vaid, *Growth and Practice of Trade Unionism* (University of Delhi, 1962), p. 141.

[3] Tucker, "Towards a Comparative Politics of Movement-Regimes," *American Political Science Review*, Vol. 55 (June 1961), p. 284.

Communist techniques and present-day practices in what was French West Africa, where Communist political and labor organizers were influential before and after World War II. But in other countries, similar techniques may be no more than a common-sense solution to the vast new problems of managing a mass society. There are undoubtedly many leaders who, if asked about the derivation of their ideologies and methods, would respond as did the early Indonesian nationalist, Tjokroaminoto, who declared that his leadership of a mass movement did not mean that he must be a Marxist or in favor of the class struggle. Remarking that, to his regret, he still had not made any study of Marxism, he then emphasized that his ideas were based on reality, not theory.[4]

It is true, however, that the success of the Communists with a particular structural and functioning model of the trade union as a mass organization could only lead to imitation. And once the Communists are in the field and use trade unions as propaganda machines and "shock troops," other political forces must meet the challenge by building a counterorganization. An Indonesian writer points out that "the non-communist socialists also understand the significance of the conception that trade unions are mass organizations. They know the advantages of this organizational principle. And they want to benefit by it as the Communists have done. And even non-socialist trade unionists, who have organized their unions along industrial lines and profit from the mass character of such unions, are, in fact, employing the same method."[5]

But it should be remembered that, as noted in an earlier chapter, the Communists themselves bowed to the nationalist fervor in these countries by adapting many of their programs and techniques in order to capitalize on it.

Coordination Between Party and Union

The typical mass movement has various other arms of specialized activity besides the unions—among them, students' and women's or-

[4] Dutch East Indies, Volksraad, Second Sitting, 1918-1919, p. 178, cited by Fred R. von der Mehden, "Marxism and Early Indonesian Islamic Nationalism," *Political Science Quarterly*, Vol. 73 (September 1958), p. 341.
[5] Iskandar Tedjasukmana, "The Political Character of the Indonesian Trade Union Movement" (Monograph Series, Modern Indonesia Project, Cornell University, 1958; multilith), pp. 75-76.

ganizations and sometimes peasant groups—but in most cases the unions are given the key role. Thus, there is need for at least a minimum of coordination between the labor wing and the political wing, although some of the political leaders worry less about coordinating with the unions than about controlling them. (The emphasis on control is of course seen particularly after independence has been won, or in a situation where unions have never had an area of genuine autonomy, as in Egypt.)

During the struggle for independence the coordination is usually loose, and the unions enjoy a considerable degree of autonomy and direct power so long as they address themselves to harassing the foreign government in power. This same pattern is seen after independence in the operations of unions that are linked to parties in opposition to a new indigenous government. The power wielded by the Moroccan UMT and the political influence of the Communist-operated SOBSI in Indonesia bear witness that militant "laborism" in pursuit of wages and better working conditions fits naturally into the total opposition pattern. The techniques are spelled out in the following excerpt from a document prepared for the January 1962 all-African Trade Union Conference in Dakar:

> It was in fact by means of our demands, made deliberately excessive in terms of domestic economic possibilities of our countries; by our violent acts including resounding strikes to support our demands; by our refusal to prepare positive solutions which, by satisfying the worker, might have integrated him into the system and thus strengthened it, that we succeeded in weakening the colonial powers.[6]

The leader of a Socialist union in India has described one of its operations in opposition to the government thus:

> Labor expected four months basic wage as bonus. The industrial court didn't give it to them. *It was obvious that there was a discontent seething among the workers. We wanted to utilize this discontent.* The elections were coming up soon and we wanted to embarrass the government and make it clear that the workers were with the Socialists. We were looking for some good occasion or issue on which the workers would heed a call from us to go on strike. This was it: so we called a "trial of strength."[7]

Recent activities of the Moroccan UMT provide an example not only of the power an opposition movement has but also of the labor

[6] Draft document prepared for consideration of the Political, Economic, and Social Committee of the Dakar Trade Union Conference, January 7-8, 1962.

[7] Quoted in Ralph James, "Politics and Trade Unions in India," *Far Eastern Survey,* Vol. 27 (March 1958), p. 43. (The italics are James's.)

eye (similar to the IWW's) that looks far beyond the confines of union membership to gain maximum political impact. In December 1961 the postal workers in Morocco staged a one-day strike for a wage increase, and also demanded that they be given greater security by being brought under legislation applicable to other government employees. A few days later the UMT called for a one-day sympathy strike of all government employees; although the move did not achieve its objectives, it amply demonstrated the widespread political implications of union activity. Among the government agencies that gave support to the UMT was the Foreign Office, sixty-eight of whose officials were discharged as a result of their participation. The Moroccan Ambassador to the United States even released a statement from Washington in support of the strikers.

Many of the activists who have been attracted to the UMT's youth and student sections are sons of businessmen and small merchants, and there is considerable hand-wringing going on in middle-class circles over the conduct of the younger generation. While in Morocco I was told of one young man who on inheriting his family business immediately sought a competent manager to take over, so that he himself could devote full time to his organizational and political activities.

In the partnerships between a union and a government newly in power, the coordination usually shows a post-independence shift in attitudes and behavior on both sides. An interesting example of this is provided by the scale of values held in the mid-1950's by the Indian INTUC in its relationship to the Congress Party (described by the citing writer in a series of questions posed in descending order of importance): (1) What does the Party want? (2) What does the government want? (3) What does the country need? (4) What do the workers need? (5) What do the workers want?[8] The author possibly overemphasized the precision of the evaluation; as a general rule union leaders are operating under conditions that do not permit such neat compartmentalization. But certainly the idea behind the scale is not untypical.

Writing in 1957, Asoka Mehta, a former trade union leader and more recently a leader of the Indian Praja Socialist Party, stated his conception of the new role of trade unions after independence most succinctly. His stand is unusual for an opposition leader, in that he stresses the sacrifices expected of organized labor in building a new state: "In underdeveloped countries . . . the chief problem is economic

[8] James, *Ibid.*

growth, and therefore the major question for unions is subordination of immediate wage gains and similar considerations to the development of the country."[9] He also saw capital accumulation as the prime goal, a viewpoint that would coincide with the opinion prevailing in the Congress Party.

Sékou Touré, President of Guinea, carried the argument even further:

> On the whole, we have the same aims. We all believe in trade unionism, but we have all understood that trade union action alone is not enough. We must use it as a political as well as an economic weapon. These are two facets of what is really the same purpose. The first problem we have to tackle is the general one of organizing unified political action through trade unions. . . . But we wanted a united African movement, taking no account of racial differences, a movement whose primary aim would be the achievement of independence, and whose secondary objective would be the safeguarding of the interests of the workers. . . . You will note that I put the political aim first, and that we are seeking to achieve it through the trade unions.[10]

President Nkrumah of Ghana has also been explicit about a union's obligation to serve the state. There are other leaders, however, such as President Tubman of Liberia, who expect greater passivity. The labor organizations may help, where they can, to provide moral support for party programs but must avoid any hint of direct action that might interfere with the government's development plans.

The changed political situation brought about by independence sometimes affects even those unions that are in opposition to the new governments, although as pointed out above the opposition role has a built-in capacity for militancy. The Trotskyite federation of labor in Ceylon, for instance, is constrained to stay within certain limits of aggression if it is to remain a force at all in the society; thus it cannot assume a stance that is blatantly anti-national. Certain Communist unions are in similar case: both the AITUC in India and the CTUF in Ceylon pay lip service to the national goals projected by the parliamentary institutions of the countries.

[9] Mehta, "The Mediating Role of the Trade Union in Under Developed Countries," *Economic Development and Cultural Change,* Vol. 6 (October 1957), p. 16.

[10] Touré, "The Republic of Guinea" (translation of an address given at Chatham House, Nov. 13, 1959), *International Affairs,* Vol. 36 (April 1960), p. 171. Subsequent to this speech, President Touré found reason to be wary of his union partners and moved to bring them under strict control; see the following section and also Chapter Seven, section on "The Need for Separation of Functions."

Strategic Position of Unions

On the basis of the above, it may seem that a good many of the labor movements are due to become helpless tools in the hands of the parties. There are many labor experts who feel that in Guinea and Ghana, especially, the trade unions have already been suborned and the labor movements deprived of any area of independent action by the structured party systems of these countries. In regard to Ghana, at least, I do not wholly agree with that analysis. Nevertheless, the threat is evident in both countries; it is also evident elsewhere, and has given rise in a number of African states to discussions on the nature of the union-party relationship. The Kenya labor federation, for example, began to examine the subject early in 1962. In Tanganyika, the federation came up with the slogan "cooperation, yes; domination, no"; nevertheless, fairly restrictive labor laws were passed by the Legislative Council in the summer of 1962.

There are, however, factors at work within the political systems of most of the developing countries which in the main will continue to give the unions certain advantages, as well as opportunities to bargain within the political complex both to their own benefit as organizations and to the benefit of their members. They will undoubtedly come under increasing controls as development progresses, but their position within the developing economy will still be strategic because a number of the factors that have operated all along to place them in a relatively favored status within the nationalist movements will continue to be important.

A great deal of a labor movement's influence in the new countries stems from its fundamental role in the transition from a traditional to a modern society. The role is not one created by the unions or imposed by the parties. It is operative before independence and after, and valid whether the unions are cooperating with government or in opposition to it. It is related to the key part played in all modern societies by industrial and urban labor forces and labor organizations, but in the developing countries the part is enhanced by the extent to which both the workers and the leaders of the organizations are needed to help mold very old social systems into very new ones. The union leaders, because of their connection with and understanding of the productive forces of a nation, are vital to development schemes; in addition, they provide the link between the laboring man and the political system. Since most of them have had some degree of formal education, and a number of them are highly educated, they are helpful in defining the elements of modernism to the rank and file of the embryo urban industrial force, which is still largely uneducated and unskilled but eager to overcome these disadvantages.

Oscar Ornati, writing in 1954, pointed up how influence of this sort was wielded by labor in India:

> The leaders and workers together form a group which has a definite im-
> pact on Indian society because its attitude is oriented toward reform and
> because of its support of educational schemes. Organized industrial work-
> ers form an important elite in the society, and the labor movement there-
> fore has a greater impact than its numerical or economic strength would
> initially lead one to expect.[11]

By 1962, however, it appeared that the Congress Party did not appre-
ciate this "elite" quality. The preparation of lists of candidates for the parliamentary elections of that year showed a tendency to disregard the recommendations made by the INTUC organizations around the country. Nevertheless, the various trade union leaders and civil servants with whom I discussed the matter in February 1962 were unani-
mous in saying that if the tendency was indeed present within the party—and admittedly there was evidence to justify such a conclusion —time and economic development would remedy the situation. The annual increment to the industrial urban work force, they predicted, would amplify labor's voice with each passing year.

An official of the railway union in Kenya provided me a simple and specific example of union assistance to the transition. I had asked him why politicians found it important to have a link with a labor organi-
zation. The response was somewhat as follows: "Union activists travel. We not only travel up and down the rail route but we also have ties with our native village. We carry news of the city to the country. We tell our friends and relatives what has happened in politics and we advise them on elections and how to vote. We have influence that extends beyond our own members—that is why we are important to the politician."

This is one of the tokens, then, which give union leaders access to the politician and to the bureaucracy. With such access to the party

---

[11] Ornati, "Indian Trade Unions Since Independence," *Far Eastern Survey*, Vol. 23 (August 1954), pp. 113-114.

mechanism, they also learn where to ask for favors and where to apply pressure to gain a desired result.

Some of the governments in power, as in Ceylon and the Ivory Coast, maintain their position by means of rural and conservative support. But despite the voting preponderance of the rural elements, it is the industrial elements of the cities that dominate the political picture at certain crucial moments. Here is where the unions find themselves in a key position, as illustrated in the following comment on the situation in Ceylon:

> Despite [competitive] labor conflict, however, the unions are so distributed in the commercial, industrial, and transport trades that they could effectively and rapidly tie up the country's economy if their leaders could agree among themselves on important strike issues that have widespread support from their rank and file. By concerted strike action they could, for example, materially influence the composition of a cabinet, the distribution of portfolios, or the direction of a government's policies.[12]

The strategic position of the trade unions within the economy is enhanced by the dearth of other interest groups or intermediate bodies capable of representing the millions of people who are emerging from the controls exerted by traditional value systems. As one of the very few such groups, a union is enabled to assume authority to speak for people far outside the confines of its own presumed membership. The entire question of how many paid-up members a union has borders on the irrelevant—so long as it is capable of stirring numbers of people to action at a given time. In Senegal the Confédération Nationale des Travailleurs Croyants (CNTC), which has only a few hundred members, is referred to as the *syndicat des cadres* because its officials are skillful bargainers and manipulators. This ability to influence events behind the screen of a miniscule organization is not unusual; there is often a difficult-to-trace relationship between a small union office located in a capital city and a strike of serious proportions many miles away.

Participation in union action is often sporadic, however, because the commitment of individual members or sympathizers to an organization is a fragile thing. They may perhaps give active support only when an issue catches their imagination or relates to their own situation. Thus the leadership of unions in opposition to a party in power is especially on the lookout for issues to exploit and methods by which

[12] W. Howard Wriggins, *Ceylon: Dilemmas of a New Nation* (Princeton University Press, 1960), p. 155.

a series of key issues can be tied together to gain maximum impact and mass support. Often, of course, loyalty can be secured simply by winning a wage increase for a given group of workers, and the stage is then set for the time when support is needed on a more obviously political issue. The Communist technique is usually to capture the support of the labor force at the outset by being the most aggressive union group in defending the rights of the worker and the most outspoken in the expression of hostility to the "bosses." This is later freely translatable into support on political matters.

Union Impact on the Political System

A labor organization working in cooperation with one of the new governments either has certain restraints imposed on its collective bargaining activities, or is expected to adopt voluntary restraints to protect the economic goals of the development plan. Obviously, a union can undertake the voluntary course much more easily when it is the only labor organization on the scene; matters become extremely difficult in a competitive union situation.

Paradoxically, the focal point of labor activity when a union is cooperating with the government shifts from employers to the interior of the political structure. The actual pressure for concessions must be directed against the government, but in a way that will not endanger its prestige. The only proper place for the discussions is at the party level, where government leaders can meet with labor leaders to thrash out the issues in dispute. An offer of future benefits sometimes convinces the union men that a moderate course is in order for the present. Recently, for instance, the secretary general of the Ghana Trade Union Congress apparently accepted restraints in the wage area in exchange for a promise of a future government-financed system of health centers to be operated under the direction of the TUC. Personal political ambitions probably played a part in his decision.

When a union's base is strong enough, it has a leverage for a type of collective bargaining within the party structure. This is seen in Africa— especially in Ghana, Guinea, and Tanganyika—where the one-party governments have moved to impose a great degree of control on the unions. Most of the labor movements have been able to function fairly well within the controls; their influence is such that the political leadership, when formulating policy, must at least calculate their attitudes and reactions. Even in Egypt, where the unions have no direct political representation, there are friends at court who speak on behalf of the workers. At the present stage of national development, representation within the political structure is more important to a union than economic bargaining power. A labor leader knows that he "can best represent the demands of his membership in political councils. This is the first fact which must be recognized by any one who wishes to understand the role of the trade union within the newly independent African societies."[13]

Granted that the unions have fallen heir to a certain amount of influence through their representation of a key group in societies emerging into modernism, this fact is in turn related to the existence of underdeveloped political systems in most of the countries. Some of the governments can be described as brittle, others as uneasily fragile.

Those that I term brittle are not without power—almost all of the African and South Asian governments can mount a great deal of power to achieve a given objective—but they have few agreed-upon techniques for replacing an administration short of coup d'états or assassinations. Any sudden shock of a nature to be felt throughout the system presents a challenge, and thus must be contained quickly. Union protest can easily become such a shock, even when the objectives of the strikers are related to economic issues. Legislation in most of the countries places some degree of restraints on strike action; therefore, any strike that does occur involves government prestige immediately, forcing government leaders to react quickly and often harshly. To delay is to run the risk of splintering the party.

The strike of the rail and dock workers in Takoradi, Ghana, in the fall of 1961 started as a spontaneous protest against a government tax policy that would have cut take-home pay substantially. The issue was quickly picked up by the surviving remnants of the political opposition to Kwame Nkrumah, with the objective, not of forcing a change of the protested policy, but of destroying the government. Even the historical mystique contained in the name "Ghana" came under attack; the opposition, operating behind the union protest, reverted to use of the pre-independence territorial name, the Gold Coast.

The Ceylon government is of the type that I term "uneasily fragile."

[13] Stephen Low, "The Role of Trade-Unions in the Newly Independent Countries of Africa," paper presented to the Research Seminar on Comparative Labor Movements, Washington, D.C., 1961. See Chapter One, footnote 6.

Composed of a party grouping which lacks any common core, it is dependent on a restless coalition of heterogeneous elements. The massed strike action that occurred in Ceylon in early 1962, with 12,000 port workers and 2,500 bank workers out, at once drove a wedge between the factions of the governing party.

One faction wanted to adopt a "soft" line toward the strikers, another, which included the Prime Minister, supported a "hard" line. When a prominent member of the Cabinet made public statements contradicting those made by the Prime Minister and other proponents of the "hard" line, the internal dissension within the government was revealed. He was pressured into retractions, but the damage was done. Furthermore, the government was caught between attacks from several left-wing parties that supported the strikers and attacks from the right-wing United National Party that charged the government with ineptitude. All of the sins of omission and commission of all the parties and their leaders over previous months were eventually dragged out for discussion before the parliament.

The unions were blessed with articulate spokesmen in the legislature who captured the floor time after time to bring the discussion back to the strike issue, despite every effort by government spokesmen to divert the debate to a more neutral subject. By the time the port workers had been out for some forty days, a first-class political crisis was in the making. Meanwhile, official "emergency rules" prohibited the newspapers from printing any strike news, except that furnished by government hand-outs. It was possible, however, to print summary despatches of the parliamentary debate; in the January 26 issue of the *Ceylon Daily News*, for example, such despatches occupied two full pages. At least 90 percent of the summarized debate pertained to the strike, and almost all of this was devoted to attacks on the government.

The entire political complex had become extremely fluid and many people predicted either the fall of the government or, at the very least, a reshuffling of the Cabinet. But when the extreme right tried to stage a coup and failed, the government regained some of its lost stature. In the appeal for unity that followed, the strikes collapsed—the Communist unions being the first to declare their loyalty—and the political situation returned to its normal fragility.[14]

I have sketched the outlines of this contretemps at some length be-

[14] In the late summer of 1962, the Ceylon government was having other troubles. See Warren Unna, "Ceylon Adrift," *Washington Post*, Sept. 4, 1962, p. A 13.

cause the tactics evidenced are typical, and because the whole affair demonstrates the value of the trade unions to a political movement, and particularly to opposition movements. The tactics are especially effective if a fine blend of economic and political issues can be produced that will appeal to the widest possible range of supporters, for it is important to build "unity of action from below." Members of and sympathizers with rival unions are brought into participation if possible, and thereby the position of rival union leaders is undercut. In the Ceylon episode, the leaders of the government-sponsored unions stood by helplessly as their meager membership was swept into support of the strikes.

Massed strike action of this sort has great impact on the political structure and weakens a government which stands on an insecure base. Each politician must reassess his position in relationship to the whole structure, and each party and party faction is likely to look about for possible new alignments and allies as accommodation is made to the challenge presented by the union action. The more loosely a government is put together, the more easily its splintering can be accomplished. A shaky coalition—such as the one that now holds government power in Kerala in South India—is particularly vulnerable to the use of unions as battering rams to precipitate a political crisis.[15]

That the effectiveness of political unionism is related in some measure to the type of political system within which it functions can be seen clearly when the consequences of strike action in the United States are compared to the events of the Ceylon crisis described above. In the United States, even lengthy strikes are in general contained within the area of industrial conflict. A state governor who opposed the union action might risk his rebid for office at the next election, but stands in no danger of being forced out before the end of his current term. Not only does the American political system itself temper the political impact of a major strike, but also a direct blow against the political structure is not envisioned by the labor unions. The various long strikes in basic steel and the auto industry, during the period since the end of World War II, have affected the political system only indirectly, if at all.

[15] Even fairly stable authoritarian regimes can be "cracked" by this technique. The 1962 strikes of miners in Spain had enough impact to elicit support from liberal Catholic elements, a factor which forced the Franco government to grant pay increases. The strikes also set the stage for further agitation on the part of those seeking to liberalize the regime.

It can be said that the labor organizations in the new countries, despite their many obvious weaknesses when evaluated by standard trade union criteria, are in many instances significant power centers. Political figures seeking mass support have responded to the generally leftward pressures generated by or emanating from the unions and from urban groups sympathetic to the claims of labor. This does not mean that all the unions are hotbeds of radicalism. It does mean that within each political complex or movement the labor groups are usually at the left of the spectrum, setting forth claims for a more egalitarian program.

The political leaders themselves, in exchange for mass support in the pre-independence period, paid much more than lip service to union claims for higher living standards and social justice, and thus in a sense made promises to the worker. After independence, because they still need the support and participation of the active urban population if the development goals of the new governments are to be met, they cannot safely ignore the promises, for the disaffection of the worker cannot be risked. On this fact rides much of the union strength. Further, the stature and utility of the labor groups, both within the political complex and within the societies, tend to be more impressive than that of the few other special-interest "modern" groups because the unions are usually better organized and have a clearer perception of their role. Perhaps most important, they have shouting power and they have access to the segments of the population which are particularly subject to manipulation and which stand most in need of social justice.

CHAPTER SEVEN

Freedom and Independence

To the extent that labor movements in Africa and Asia are part of larger political movements it is obvious that the phrase "free and independent trade unionism" is ambiguous, if used within the American frame of reference. All of the trade unions in the new nations are subject to substantial restraints in carrying on relations with employers in the exercise of their economic function. Nearly all are connected with political forces or political figures whose broadly inclusive objectives often run counter to the more narrow purposes of the "pure" trade union. A good many unions appear to be party captives, and certain others, which started as quasi-independent centers of power, may be approaching this state.

This is the generalized picture. Within it can be found a wide variety of specific pictures, which, if considered only from a distance, appear in their turn to fall more or less neatly into several categories, similar to those suggested in the spectrum experimentally outlined in Chapter One. But the categories are too general to be of service to analysis, unless each one of the relationships between the unions and the parties has first been studied as a thing in itself. Though it cannot be denied that all of the relationships curtail the independence of the labor movements in some degree, each specific case of restraint or captivity represents a subtle combination of circumstances not duplicated by any other. When the cases are, not categorized, but compared it becomes apparent that such a word as "captivity" is relative to a number of variables and far too inexact to describe all of the facets of the situations to which it is applied.

The four specific relationships described briefly below are cited as examples, not types; they were chosen from the many discussed throughout, because, when put in conjunction, they illustrate the range of variations well. The second and third differ widely from the first and fourth and seem to resemble each other, but close examination shows that they are two specific variations on a theme that was prevalent in Africa in the early 1960's.

Examples of Union-Party Relationships

THE INDIAN NATIONAL TRADE UNION CONGRESS has enjoyed a large measure of autonomy in conducting its internal affairs, and there is no political commissar riding herd on it. But in a showdown the Congress Party is dominant. The general community of interest between union leaders and Congress Party leaders has so far been sufficient to keep the union from adopting a wholly independent line. There was, for example, no move within INTUC to join the strike of government employees in the summer of 1960, even though INTUC's wage claims were similar to those of the Socialist HMS, the prime mover in calling the strike.

THE GHANA TRADE UNION CONGRESS is not free from or independent of the Convention Peoples Party and the personal mandate of President Nkrumah. The TUC leadership has no desire to break the political tie at this time; therefore the officers of the federation had no choice, if they wished to hold onto their jobs, but to fight the protest strikes set off in the fall of 1961 by workers in Takoradi. The lines running between the CPP and the government and those between the CPP, the government, and the TUC are direct, with no buffers which might mask the types of pressures mounted against the unions. Conversely, these direct lines often work to the advantage of the TUC. Its secretary general, for instance, sits as a member of the CPP Executive Council and attends Cabinet meetings; as an official, he has had more personal power, at least until recently, than some of the Cabinet members. Despite restraints, the unions continue to function as strong and well-organized interest groups.

IN SENEGAL, the union leaders are not free from government interference, although the types of controls are more subtle and usually more indirect than in Ghana. Not always, however: in late 1959 the government moved in to break the strike of government employees, and some of the workers who were fired at that time have still not been rehired. President Senghor has stated his conception of the unions' responsibility to the state—cooperation with government in building the nation—in terms not too different from those of President Sékou Touré of Guinea, although in general a more permissive atmosphere prevails in Senegal than in Guinea. Union leaders are called before government officials and told bluntly what they can do and what is prohibited, but since much of this goes on behind the scenes the appearance of harmony is not dispelled.

So far the labor leaders in Senegal have not risen up in rebellion. They subscribe to the goals of the government and, though they may at times chafe at the restrictions imposed or in some cases wait impatiently for their day in the sun to arrive, they volunteer their services and those of their organizations to the total movement.

This concern for the success of the total independence movement was strikingly illustrated in a paper prepared for the 1962 Dakar Trade Union Congress by a union leader who was in exile for trade union activities "incompatible" with official attitudes:

> Just as we supported the struggle of the African people against colonial exploitation, we must refrain from any activity which might harm the maintenance and reinforcement of that independence. . . . [We must] draw up and support a constructive plan of work for the young African nations in the process of development. . . . [The primary responsibility for the task of planning rests with governments and parties, but] in view of the fact that the struggle against colonialism found its justification in the concepts of liberty, democracy, and progress, there is ample grounds to demand that the various social elements have the opportunity to present their interests during the formulation of the plan.

He concluded by emphasizing a factor that provides the unions whatever leverage they are to have in the immediate future: "Political considerations advise the same approach."[1]

THE ISRAELI HISTADRUT operates under circumstances that are uniquely different from those of nearly all other labor federations in the new countries. It is a highly centralized union movement within a highly centralized political framework. It plays an equally distinctive role within the society, for it has taken on a large part of the responsibility of building the society. Conceptually, it is close to the objectives explicitly stated by union leaders in Africa and to the unstated but implicit objectives of those in South Asia. Established before the State

---

[1] The writer of this paper was an exile from Guinea, not Senegal, but his views on the need for responsible interest-group participation in development planning are typical of those of well-educated labor leaders in most of the countries.

of Israel existed, Histadrut acquired tremendous power by undertaking many of the functions ordinarily exercised by a government. Much of the present tension between the federation and the government is a product of the latter's determination to take over these functions. A large part of the Histadrut-operated educational system has been transferred to government auspices; operation of the employment offices is now wholly in the hands of the state; and in early 1962 there was talk of a take-over of the Histadrut health services.

In addition, employer and other interest groups are beginning to challenge the long dominance of Histadrut. The separation of economic classes by function is now fairly well advanced, and professional groups—including teachers and engineers—are questioning the egalitarian wage policies of the past. Histadrut is also no longer the only source of political recruitment. In sum, the political system of Israel is in a period of transition; as a consequence, changes are taking place within the labor movement. Histadrut is due at long last to lose some of its power, in common with many unions in other new countries that have lost varying amounts of their influence. For most of the latter, however, the loss came more quickly.

Whatever the end product of the transition in Israel, Histadrut is clearly not going to become a servile captive of the government or of a party. It will remain one of the major special-interest groups in the country, and is not likely to turn to an opposition role simply because its function has been modified. Part of its central strength lies in its sustained and highly creative "labor nationalism"; in contrast to many of the African unions, Histadrut has never sacrificed its labor orientation to the service of pure nationalism.

In this it has much in common with the long-established labor groups in Europe, especially those in Scandinavia, that are functionally related to various Social Democratic and Labor parties. This European relationship pattern merits discussion here, because the factors that brought it into being show the other side of the coin of political unionism and demonstrate to some extent why certain European labor movements were able to take a course different from that now being taken by most of the unions in the new nations.[2]

---

[2] I first explored these factors in a paper, "The Relationship of the Norwegian Labor Party to the Trade-Unions," prepared for the Research Seminar on Comparative Labor Movements. See Chapter One, footnote 6.

Union-Party Relationships in West Europe

The Social Democratic and the Labor parties of western Europe originally emerged from movements which, incorporating a broad representational front of interest groups, centered their activities on improving the lot of the classes in the society that suffered most from economic deprivation and political repression. Civil and political rights ranked high in the system of values the movements hoped to implement. The political parties that came into being were prepared to give (or in some cases were forced to do so by later developments) a high degree of independent life to the trade unions associated with them.

The Norwegian labor federation (LO), for example, owes its organizational independence to the circumstance that, when the Norwegian Labor Party encouraged its establishment in 1899, some of the leaders of the affiliating unions and substantial segments of their membership had ties with the Liberal Party and would have refused affiliation with a federation that was an integral part of a competing party. Even though the LO is today functionally united with the Labor Party, the principle of organizational independence is still taken for granted by party leaders and union leaders alike.

The large measure of autonomy the Norwegian LO enjoys is fairly typical of that granted to most of the union movements which are linked to the Social Democratic and Labor parties in various other countries of western and northern Europe. Among a number of factors that can be pinpointed as accounting for the general tendency, two have special relevance in contrast to factors now operating on union-party relationships in Asia and Africa.

First, the political forces represented by the European Socialists were in organized opposition to government for a long time during the latter part of the nineteenth century and the early twentieth. Thus, over a much longer period than was available to most of the indigenous movements in opposition to the colonial governments of Asia and Africa, the coordination of policies between the unions and the parties could be relatively loose, and the unions were in general able to develop their own policies on industrial matters.

Second, at the time the party-union relationships were evolving in the West European countries, the respective national economies were for the most part fairly well developed. Therefore a target existed for industrial relations activity through which improved wage and working conditions could be extracted. The inherent logic of the situation called for a trade union arm that functioned *as* a trade union—and the parties recognized the logic. In carrying out this specialized function, the union leadership sometimes grew in influence to the point of being able to challenge the party leadership. It was also not unusual for a union with a well-established dues-collection system to become the chief financial contributor to its related party.

The basis and the effects of the union-party relationship in these movement structures can be seen most clearly in examples from the Scandinavian countries, where the pattern is most marked and perhaps most successful. The tie between the trade union federation and the Social Democratic Party in Sweden has been described as follows:

> . . . the union-Party relationship was [at first] one of inter-dependence . . . [but] this relation changed with the passage of time in response to changing economic and political conditions and the very growth of the labor movement itself. These circumstances required greater specialisation of function, and hence specialisation and differentiation of union and Party organizations.[3]

The division of functions is also important in Norway. It was well defined by the vice chairman of the Norwegian Labor Party in an address to the LO's 1957 convention:

> The organizations which are represented here are a good expression of the breadth of the Norwegian labor movement, and the good, open co-operation which exists between these organizations contributes to create the milieu and the climate which gives us the possibilities of a progressive policy. . . . The actual situation is that these two organizations [the party and the federation] through tradition and mature consideration have divided the labor tasks between themselves.[4]

This characteristic concept of "division of tasks" did not spring from the minds of men in a fully developed form in Sweden, Norway, or other West European countries. Its evolution was, as noted earlier, re-

---

[3] Donald J. Blake, *Swedish Trade Unions and the Social Democratic Party: the Formative Years* (Reprint No. 166, Institute of Industrial Relations, University of California, 1961), pp. 43-44.

[4] Trygve Bratteli, Address to the 1957 Convention of the Norwegian Federation of Labor, in *Protokoll Over Kongressen* (official record of the convention), p. 26. The representation mentioned by Bratteli included, besides members of the unions and the Labor Party, guest groups from the Socialist youth movement, the labor press, and the workers' educational association.

lated in part to the development of the economy, and in part to the consolidation of certain political currents. In Norway, for instance, it was not a matter of legal principle or a constitutional formulation on the part of the party or the federation; it was an outgrowth of a cultural milieu, and in some part an application of ethical principles derived from historical experience common to the West. But even though the concept was nurtured in a social complex so different from that of the now-developing countries, it could possibly constitute a guide for the management of union-party relationships in the Asian and African situations where successful relationships are vastly important to national development.

Centripetal vs. Centrifugal Forces

Most of the new countries are at a stage of development that prohibits their political leaders from giving much present attention to such niceties of political management as the Scandinavian union-party relationships. They are busy with the enormous task of accumulating sufficient power to keep them in control of the political machinery; at the same time they are applying at least some of the social cement needed to hold the country in one piece as a nation. The centrifugal forces almost equal the centripetal. It is small wonder that some of these harried men—even when they have had a trade union background —see a labor movement, with its massed power base and its capacity for organization, not as a former partner in the liberation struggle but as a possible source of political competition and an even more possible threat to economic development plans. Thus the measures designed to curb the unions are, in a sense, recognition of their actual or potential power within the context of a fluid political situation.

The trend in Africa toward highly centralized political systems and governments is already established, and in many instances may represent an absolute necessity. In any event, the trend cannot be easily arrested or reversed, for the politicians in power are intent on remaining in power. But their power is still not sufficient to make them sure they can contain opposition, and so opposition is their greatest fear. They believe that success after winning independence "hinges on their ability to demonstrate in the early days of their autonomy the ability to weld together the diverse tribal, clan, racial, and other groupings into a nation without false starts or temporary setbacks. The urgent necessity for sustained unity is perhaps the central concern of the power elite in each new African nation."[5]

The centralization of the political structure is usually reflected in the union structure, and all the more so because the union-building process in recent years has usually been from the top down. The trend toward centralization is seen even in such presumably moderate political systems as those of Tanganyika and Senegal. Both of these states have moved in the direction of greater labor controls because it is now accepted gospel that free trade unionism may endanger economic planning and political stability.

The trend is not so apparent in India and in Ceylon where the political rationale is more permissive. However, Selig S. Harrison has pointed out that "Nehru's leadership focuses more and more plainly on a single over-riding objective: to assert a dominant centralizing power before the claims of regional self-interest can gather momentum." In a later study, Harrison suggests that basic changes, presumably those leading to greater centralization, must be effected if India is to progress.[6]

A Middle Ground?

What then are the proper types of relationship between the unions and the political parties? There is no precise answer. As must be obvious by now, I feel strongly that the outsiders who are working to encourage development in the new countries must rid themselves of the restrictions inherent in the "free and independent unionism" slogan, with its built-in bias for the American type of collective bargaining. At the same time, I abhor the possibility that the politicians in some of these countries might find it expedient to eliminate all areas of freedom for interest groups in general and the trade unions in particular. This is not at all a remote possibility, should a state decide to speed up economic growth through essentially totalitarian methods.

Some, at least, of the political leaders, enviously scanning the development record of the Soviet Union, may very well feel that this is the only route for them to travel in view of the serious and multitudi-

[5] Hugh H. Smythe and Mabel M. Smythe, "Black Africa's New Power Elite," *South Atlantic Quarterly*, Vol. 59 (Winter 1960), pp. 22-23.

[6] Harrison, "The Challenge to Indian Nationalism," *Foreign Affairs*, Vol. 34 (July 1956), p. 620, and *India, the Most Dangerous Decades* (Princeton University Press, 1960), Chap. 8.

nous obstacles they face—overlooking (or choosing to ignore) that the price in political terms of completely destroying the autonomy of these highly useful groups could be too high in the long run. Certainly, this is not the type of political development the western democracies can encourage, even if they can be sympathetically tolerant toward the short-run expediency of limiting individual and organizational freedom more than democratic custom approves.

I am personally more than dubious of attempts to transfer western political institutions intact to societies steeped in other traditions. However, once the concept of nationhood (which is quite different from nationalism) has rooted itself more substantially, I believe it may be possible to encourage the indigenous directors of political development to seek channels which in turn will encourage pluralism—even when the pluralism must be registered within the confines of a single-party political system. Perhaps the present-day form of the systems is less important than the course that will be followed as these new political entities evolve further.

A fairly high degree of centralization in political and trade union structures need not, for instance, be considered bad per se. Similarly, the political affiliations of the unions can be understood as a normal response to the situation and, in many cases, a salutary one. In the case of India, the nature of the present relationship between the Congress Party and INTUC could be improved upon, but the fact that the relationship exists at all is a positive element in the total political complex. No American observer would, I am sure, suggest that the Indian labor force be turned over to complete Communist domination, yet no union movement that prevents such domination by competing with the Communist AITUC could survive without political support. In certain other countries where the unions are cooperating with government, observers may justifiably lament the extent to which the labor arm is subservient. Nevertheless, overemphasis by outsiders on a more militant bargaining role for the unions might very well push some of them into undertaking the kind of lone-wolf opposition role that easily becomes vulnerable to exploitation, either by the Communists or by traditionalists in the society who wish to thwart the new governments.

In sum, to disregard the present-day realities of these labor movements could be disastrous. Therefore, the area of discussion for western advisers must center around the realities, and not around an abstract notion of freedom related to other labor organizations that came into being under very different circumstances in a social setting which was at a very different stage of development. There must be a middle ground as a vantage point from which to determine how many of the postulates advanced by the new governments regarding the unions are truly axiomatic. As a prime example, there is need for discussion of the continuing tendency among many African and Asian economic planners to calmly accept the idea that union wage demands pose an absolute threat to economic development. Like many generalizations, this one has sufficient relevance to give it a convincing ring, but it actually calls for an examination in depth.

Consumption vs. Capital Accumulation

The dichotomy posed by economists, both within the new countries and outside, and accepted by many of the political leaders pits accumulation of capital against increases in consumption. Wage increases are said to spur the latter and reduce the former. As a blanket theory, this is not necessarily true. If, for instance, an increase in money earnings granted to an undernourished labor force is spent on food—as it most likely would be—productivity of the labor force might rise. The economic plans of most of the developing countries include measures to increase agricultural production. Should the measures meet with success, the potentially inflationary effect of wage increases would to some extent be reduced. Similarly, since a portion of increased wages could be expected to go for clothing, the existence of surplus textile capacity in such countries as India and Egypt should act as a curb on inflation.

Two other relevant factors are pointed out by economist Paul Fisher:

(1) Since a relatively small proportion of the labor force in the less-developed countries is affected by successful union efforts to raise the wage level, it would seem rash to credit labor unions with the ability to increase substantially the general consumption level. . . . Wage gains of one-half of 1 per cent of the population do not easily affect the total consumption level. (2) Most union wage drives aim at restoring the worker's wage eroded by inflation.[7]

A too ready acceptance of the consumption versus capital accumulation theory would seem capable of producing its own specific obstacles

[7] Fisher, "The Economic Role of Unions in Less-Developed Areas," *Monthly Labor Review*, Vol. 84 (September 1961), pp. 953-954.

to further development. The right wing of a political spectrum frequently promulgates blanket statements regarding the link between wage rises, inflation, and the subsequent loss of capital funds. Such statements should be subjected to close analysis in each given situation. Although general wage and consumption levels may need to be dampened, economic development is inevitably uneven, and workers who are in favored spots of the economy should derive at least some advantage therefrom in the form of small wage improvements.

In the policy arguments about permitting the unions to pursue limited wage claims for their members, one important aspect of the matter is often overlooked by the politicians. There are, after all, limits to a union's ability to hold the wage line in the face of pressures from below. In the countries where multiple unionism is the rule, such pressures are especially strong; a pro-government union that is prohibited from operating in the area of wages and benefits is bound to have a good many of its members picked up by the Communists. But in any of the countries, a union leader who indefinitely evades response to agitation by the membership for improvements risks losing his position of leadership and thereby his usefulness to the party and/or the government. In the long run the whole political movement may be the loser if the labor arm eventually withdraws its political support and its notably progressive influence.

Most of the governments in power realize to some extent that economic development cannot take place without a favorable social and political climate. But they often fail to recognize the corollary: to achieve such a climate, some flexibility in the wage area must be permitted and some risk of inflation must be taken. After all, the labor leaders are in general committed to the same development goals as the political leaders. So long as they are aligned with the governments in power, they can usually be trusted to urge moderation on the union membership.

There are times, however, when it is emphatically not feasible for union leaders to work counter to membership demands for improvements in wages and working conditions. The governments and the parties must face up to this fact, but some of them have not yet learned to do so. On the other hand, since the union leaders are in the best position to know when worker dissatisfaction has reached crisis proportions, they are betraying their commitment to the national goals if they do not insist on retaining enough independence to speak out honestly and bluntly within party caucuses at such a time. In certain instances "immediate satisfaction of urgent consumption demands might be necessary to prevent political or social upheavals. In that situation the increase of consumption is the price to be paid to avert a further deterioration of the prospect for economic growth."[8]

The Permanent Dialogue

One of the most interesting ideas voiced at the January 1962 Dakar trade union conference was that of the "permanent dialogue" within the framework of the one-party—or virtually one-party—systems in Africa. The idea was offered as the rationale that lends legitimacy to this particular form of government: debate would continue, but in each case the single party is, presumably, designed to limit the conflict to manageable proportions. One analyst assesses the idea as follows:

> How far this ideal of government by discussion has actually been realized, in the FLN or any other African political organization, deserves investigation. But that it is an operative idea in many of the mass parties is undeniable. And, as . . . pointed out in relation to the French West African parties, insofar as the idea has been applied, it has operated as a barrier to the influence of external pressure-groups upon the party, assisted the resolution of internal controversies, made it easier to deal with problems of succession within the leadership, and provided some check upon corruption and patronage.[9]

Despite such judgments, there is clear-cut evidence that debate from the trade union side is subject to more and more restraints, in Guinea and Ghana especially, but elsewhere as well—including states in Asia. In Egypt, for instance, the dialogue has never been a serious one. In India, where the issue of trade union freedom is not in question per se, if there is any dialogue between INTUC and the upper ranks of the Congress Party it is unimpressive, since the federation is more or less taken for granted by the party and sometimes therefore hampered in competing with the Communist AITUC.

Continued vitality of the movements for national development demands a meaningful dialogue within all the varieties of the political enclaves, and one which allows for conflicting points of view. Even though consensus is the transcendent goal, there is great value in conflict so long as a given point under dispute does not challenge certain

---

[8] Adolph Sturmthal, "Unions and Economic Development," *Economic Development and Cultural Change*, Vol. 8 (January 1960), p. 204.

[9] Thomas Hodgkin, *African Political Parties* (Penguin Books, 1961), p. 100.

basic institutional factors. The present tendency in Africa to discard this value by closing out the debate at will and limiting the circle of those permitted to contribute to plans and policies is unfortunate. At stake is not only the freedom of the unions but also, and possibly more importantly, the degree of independent life to be enjoyed by the other associational interest groups now in being and those which will emerge later. Decisions affecting the labor movements could set a pattern affecting all manner of social institutions in the future.

At present, however, the unions as a rule constitute a powerful interest group, and their leaders are articulate spokesmen for a point of view. Since the actions of some of the leaders at times imply political competition, it is understandable that political leaders may feel it urgent to apply restraints, although to an outsider not cognizant of all the factors involved, such a step might appear unnecessary. If it is necessary, it would seem imperative that the governments and the parties find a mechanism and an ethic which will still allow a degree of internal autonomy for this important group.

The Need for Separation of Functions

As pointed out earlier, most of the governments are too young and too conscious of their weaknesses to pay much heed at this time to developmental theories which predicate a high degree of individual or organizational freedom. Nevertheless, it is not too soon for informed outsiders to start a "dialogue" from their side of the fence with union, party, and government leaders who are grappling with these problems. The approach should not purport to sell anything for immediate consumption. The dialogue must avoid sloganeering about freedom and independence for this or that individual union or labor movement; the ideas introduced must relate to the present-day realities faced by the political and trade union leaders of all the countries. Most important, the dialogue must be conducted between friendly equals.

Just as it is possible to find a middle ground for discussing consumption versus capital accumulation, so too there can be a middle ground for discussing the role of interest groups in general, and of trade unions in particular. At present, a joint examination of this issue by those of us from the West and the concerned groups of the new countries would perhaps be highly theoretical and abstract. Nevertheless, it might point the way to a future political development that can envision a loosening of restraints. It has been my experience, even in localities considered to be aggressively anti-American, that such exchanges can be mutually useful.

One of the problems to be examined in such a dialogue is the tendency of political unionism in these countries to commingle the economic function and the political function. The tendency evolved in the early stages of both trade unionism and political activism; it was, and probably still is, advantageous to both endeavors during periods of impending crisis. But for the long-term drive toward national development, such an intimate mix of functions may be a severe handicap.

In both Ghana and Guinea, for example, the labor movements have developed a type of party within a party. Over time, as more and more of the union activities take on the appearance of political activities, a union also takes on the appearance of a competitor to the party. Although the party chief is still dominant, the union's course puts him under pressure. The structuring of the party-union relationship permits him to restrain the unions, even to a point where they become mere appendages without an internal life of their own. There is no "fence" to separate the party function from the union function, and vice versa. Under such circumstances, the party may then try to carry on some of the industrial functions of the unions, an attempt that rashly courts disaster.

An example of what I am talking about is provided by events that took place in Guinea in 1961. The Guinea labor federation (CNTG) had for some time been using its relatively great autonomy to conduct its own competitive brand of politics, of which the high point was the virtual domination of the Ministry of Labor by the CNTG's Secretary General Kaba. Thus goaded, President Touré used the incident of the "Teachers' Crisis" of November 1961 as the rationale for removing all vestiges of autonomy from the CNTG, and has seemingly had the political situation under control since then. However, by thus shackling the intellectuals represented by the teachers union and the workers represented by the CNTG, he may have struck a body blow to long-run development.

It is interesting that as early as 1952 the importance of separating functions was stressed by S. A. Dange, the Indian Communist leader and secretary general of the AITUC. For four years prior to that time the Communists had used the "hard line" in India, a maneuver that was almost disastrous for the party. At a conference of CP members.

Dange pointed out the two major mistakes that had been made in those years: union work and party work were almost identical, despite warnings of the International on this score, and mass trade union activity had been given up "in the name of the politicalisation of the working class."[10]

It seems certain that sound political development in the new countries must be posited on the evolution of cooperative relationships between the political parties in power and the special-interest groups—including the few that now exist and others that, hopefully, may develop later. A prerequisite to this is the separation of functions, although it probably cannot be achieved in the immediate future. For the present, however, in regard to the party-union relationships, even rudimentary steps toward developing a distinct trade union wing and a distinct political wing within a total political structure would be an improvement over the present scrambled picture.

In a relevant division of the enormous number of tasks that must be accomplished before the new societies can be actually viable, the area marked out for the trade unions would contain a host of operations, relating to (1) the economic function that is the common franchise of labor movements and (2) the political and social functions that are important to national development. In the first category, the unions must represent their members in the wage field; taking into account the known issues, this can probably be best accomplished by carefully negotiating a set of cooperative guide lines within the party and government structure. There is also a big job to be done in handling the kinds of grievances and plant issues that do not involve increases in money wages.

In the second category, the unions could very well take on, at relatively low monetary cost, the vastly important task of adult education and some of the vocational training load, while the government concentrates on the staggering challenge of general education. There are numerous other needed social efforts of this sort which are especially appropriate to labor movements. In carrying them out, the unions would be strengthening their own institutional image, as well as contributing directly to national development.

[10] Dange, *On the Indian Trade Union Movement,* a report to the Convention of Communist Party Members Working in the Trade Union Movement, Calcutta. May 20-22, 1952 (Communist Party Publication, printed at Bombay), p. 51.

Any treatment of the future role and position of the trade unions within the evolving political systems of the developing countries is bound to seem unfinished and inconclusive. There are no definitive and neat prescriptions for the most advantageous and workable relationship between trade unions, political parties, and governments. There is certainly no single ideal solution. It is possible, however, to suggest that a variety of solutions can be found, if the search for them is based realistically on the specific needs of an individual country projected against a background of the problems common to all of the countries.

As the next chapter will point out, many of the unions, through the performance of tasks especially suited to their vantage point in the society, have made specific contributions to political modernization and the national development. If less restrained by their political partners, they might be capable of contributing a great deal more. One of the large problems faced by the political forces, then, is how best to utilize the services of the unions for constructive ends.

CHAPTER EIGHT

The Union Contribution to Development

WHEN ONE SETS OUT TO ASSESS the social significance of trade union operations in the new countries, certain difficulties are at once encountered. The effectiveness and utility of the union role of course vary from country to country; therefore generalizations are subject to challenge, since none would apply equally in all instances. The fluid political situation and the changes in the union role also make it perilous to assume that a blanket statement in the present tense will hold beyond tomorrow—and even more perilous to indulge in predictions. Certain contours that emerge when one scans the over-all scene have much in common, but to claim any greater likeness than this is to risk being in error. I have, however, taken that risk at times.

The point to be made here is indicated by the fact that I use "contribute," not as a value word, but in the simple sense of "adding to." Thus, a specific factor that the unions have added to the development process of their respective countries is not necessarily a good; although it may prove to be one under given future circumstances, it could also turn out to be the opposite. Similarly, a certain contribution may be valuable at one time—say during the struggle for independence—and detrimental at a later time.

It is my own belief that much that the labor movements have added to their societies has value, but the permanence of the value depends not only on the unions themselves, according to what future course they take, but also on other elements in the society. At this writing, however, there is evidence that the unions have made contributions by assisting political development and social integration; by helping to counter communism; by managing worker protest in the interests of national development. My treatment of each of these wide areas is necessarily sketchy, but may serve (1) to call attention to the areas where outside encouragement of unionism can be helpful and where it cannot, and (2) to re-emphasize that any encouragement must be geared to the realities of the given political and economic situation.

Contribution to Political Development

POLITICAL EDUCATION. In nearly all of the countries, the labor organizations have been in some degree instrumental in providing a most necessary prerequisite to popular participation in the politics of independence—a heightened political consciousness among the urban population. Undoubtedly, this contribution hastened the coming of independence in a number of cases. It can be questioned whether, as a consequence, some of the new states had a sufficient period of incubation, but this is mostly a question asked by westerners of other westerners, and only serves to make the intentions of all westerners somewhat suspect to the Africans and Asians.

There are certain more realistic bases for questioning the value of the contribution. In many instances it has led to a type of extremism which could bode ill for the future if the trade unions use their mass power after independence in a disruptive fashion. As an example, the attempts made by the labor federation in Guinea to usurp the role of the political party would have, if not checked, worked counter to sound political development in the long run. Again, in countries where the major union federation is Communist-dominated, its political-education contribution to the political system is dubious. The Indonesian SOBSI is such a case. Being tied to the local Communist party, its long-term goal can almost certainly be nothing other than harmful to constructive political development, inasmuch as the political parent has an ultimate goal that includes arresting such development at a certain point and imposing its own solution. The non-Communist unions in Indonesia are weak and for the most part ineffective. At this stage, their contribution is limited in the main to the fact of their existence, which at least denies the Communists complete control over the labor force. They cannot be expected to do much more than this unless a sufficient degree of consensus emerges among Indonesia's political leadership to permit some consolidation of the political forces—from which could stem a more cohesive union structure.

Many more examples could be cited to illustrate the possible difficulties when unions are cast in the role of political educator. Nevertheless, I believe that, to date, this aspect of the labor movements' role has been valuable in most cases. Those who will agree with me are conceding, as I am, that the gaining of independence is a good thing in and by itself. To the extent that the unions contributed to the independence campaigns through political education—and this is a variable factor—I can only conclude that the endeavor was in keeping with the over-all needs of the society and therefore a constructive use of union power in the interests of the people.

Obviously, independence was a necessary first step before genuine political development could begin. The suddenness of its arrival in some cases, however, has resulted in a slowing up of the next stage, and therefore the administration of a good many of the countries is faulty and confused. Yet millions of Africans and Asians regard the economic opportunities that have increasingly opened for them as proof enough that independence is more important than good administration.

The economic bargaining power of these millions of people and many of their other relationships to the society no longer involve issues of race or political dependency. Foreign commercial interests have been hastening to train Africans for jobs previously held by Europeans. In Ceylon the tea plantations are now using local personnel in assistant manager jobs, which earlier were reserved for Europeans; chances for native ownership of plantations are also on the rise. Another bonus being felt in nearly every country is the now wide-open opportunity for government employment—and beyond that the dazzling idea of access to one level or another of political power. All of this has meant a psychic enrichment so great that it probably can never be measured.

Psychological barriers have also gone down for the unions themselves. Under the colonial administrations the carrying out of genuine collective bargaining, for example, was hampered by the existence of institutional forms predicated on the political, economic, and social superiority of the managerial class. So long as these forms persisted it was inevitable that management attitudes would be hostile to collective bargaining and that, despite sincere attempts of the colonial administrators to develop trade unions, the home governments and the colonial administrations would tend to reinforce the position of management. The political implications of early union activity made for distrust between government officials and labor movement leaders, impeding on both sides the development of cooperative attitudes.

For the people in general and for trade union leaders and members the new political forms can, over time and with luck, be a stimulus to the growth of political maturity and responsibility. In any case the unions have not finished with their job as political educators; some of the new phases of the job will be discussed later in this chapter.

PROVISION OF POLITICAL LEADERSHIP. A great many of the party leaders, government administrators on various levels, and members of parliament are products of the labor movements' "talent reservoirs."

Among those who rose to top-level power in Africa through the trade union route are Sékou Touré, President of Guinea; Cyrille Adoula, Prime Minister of the Congo; Sir Roy Welensky, Prime Minister of the Federation of Rhodesia and Nyasaland; Josh Nkomo, leader of the nationalist forces in Southern Rhodesia; Rachidid Kawawa, Prime Minister of Tanganyika; M. Kamalizi, Minister of Labor in Tanganyika; Tom Mboya, formerly secretary general of the Kenya African National Union Party and more recently Minister of Labor; Abdoulaye Ba, head of the Senegalese Eastern Regional Assembly and member of the National Assembly. There are also hundreds of union men among the less-noted officials who carry on political or governmental responsibilities. In French West Africa in 1958, for example, union leaders held portfolios in the governments of seven out of the eight territories.[1] The Moroccan UMT, at present shut out of posts at the national level, has placed a good many of its officials as members of municipal councils in the major cities, and especially in Casablanca and Rabat.

In some parts of Asia, probably because of the greater number of trained political leaders and civil servants there who derive from the longer experience with political institutions and practices, the trade union route to power is less pronounced, but still evident. In India there are a number of prominent past and present party leaders and Cabinet ministers whose start in public affairs was the union movement. Among them are Gulzarilal Nanda, Minister of Labor and Minister of Planning; Khandubhai Desai, former head of the Textile Labor Association and former Minister of Labor; and V. V. Giri (from the railway unions), also a former Minister of Labor and presently governor of Kerala State. Although neither Gandhi nor Nehru can be said to owe his rise to his work in the labor movement, Nehru served as head of the AITUC before it became a Communist instrument and Gandhi organized the Textile Labor Association and was for a time its leader. Both of these men saw the trade union, not in its industry-

---

[1] Thomas Hodgkin, *African Political Parties* (Penguin Books, 1961), p. 119.

oriented function, but as a mechanism to extend their political and moral influence.

Myron Weiner, in his study of Indian politics, accurately shows the predominant political influence of the intellectual, professional, and middle classes. But he goes on to say that the Indian parties have difficulty in recruiting active membership from the unions, and backs this up by stating that of 469 active Praja Socialist Party members surveyed in the city of Bombay, 136 were industrial workers.[2] His figures bring me to an opposite conclusion—that the Indian unions are indeed one of the important areas of political recruitment.

In Africa it is probable, as the political job channels become less open and recruitment and training become available through more varied sources, that fewer labor leaders will be called on. If so, the unions would be strengthened in several ways, for they have suffered from the loss of some of their most effective leaders to the political sector. If the labor men find that there is a diminishing need for their services in political posts, and are thereby forced to recognize that their futures depend on ability to carry on the trade union function, continuity may again be restored to the union leadership.

POLITICAL MODERNIZATION. The unions have been front-running participants in the radical shifting of the societies from "old" to "new," most of which has taken place amid hortatory incitement to even more rapid change. During such a breakdown and modification of established customs and mores, especially when the former political authority has been highly autocratic, the "rapid and violent displacement of that authority by a democratic regime is highly favorable to the emergence of extremist mass movements that tend to transform the new democracy in anti-democratic directions."[3] In many regions of Africa and Asia the spoor of extremist movements is seen in schemes bearing such titles as "Guided Democracy" and in the frequent resort to preventive detention laws.

In most instances the new governments are striving to gain some degree of political consensus on how to get on with the job of modernizing their political and economic systems. The unions are the natural partners of political forces with this goal in mind, partly because they are the intermediary between the political complex and the labor force—and it is on the labor force that a large part of the

[2] Weiner, *Party Politics in India* (Princeton University Press, 1957), p. 232.
[3] William Kornhauser, *The Politics of Mass Society* (Free Press, 1959), p. 125.

modernizing effort must depend. But perhaps even more important is the fact that the functionally oriented and organized operation of a non-Communist labor movement is to a certain extent a demonstration of democratically motivated modernization and therefore a likely counter to the anti-democratic directions of the extremist movements. An outsider may find it difficult to perceive the modernism, since the union membership is more often than not fragmented, short on skills, and in some cases still in search of an industry to justify its name of "labor force." Nevertheless, for a great number of the union's members the union's direct representation of their economic and political interests constitutes their first participation in a modern organization—and one that relates them to an ever-broadening social pattern.

As supporters and often initiators of economic and political modernization, the unions may be crass in their methods at times—moving too fast or wanting to do too many things at once. This does not diminish their importance as instruments of change.

> It is particularly in the early stages of economic development, when the resistance of a traditional society has to be overcome, when the necessary institutional changes—for instance, doing away with an archaic land tenure system or an inequitable tax system or reforming the educational system—spell success or failure of all economic measures, that the union's support of the reform forces appears indispensable. Where the body politic is in the hands of the vested interests of a minority, the mass (mob) demonstration and extralegal pressure on society becomes one of the most powerful means of bringing about a peaceful change. For this role the union is eminently equipped. Its basic attitude is directed to a change for the better, toward progress.[4]

Social Integration

Until recently, the substantial part played by the labor organizations in integrating the labor force and other elements of the population into the new type of society (which the unions have also been helping to build) has probably been incidental to more pressing necessities. To win independence was the first necessity, and the second was to make independence meaningful through the establishment of a strong state. For both missions, a political force had to be built. When the unions brought their mass organization technique to bear on the task, the participation of the masses in winning independence was a first step in a new social integration.

[4] Paul Fisher, "The Economic Role of Unions in Less-Developed Areas," *Monthly Labor Review*, Vol. 84 (September 1961), p. 956.

In view of the change in union relationships to the parties since independence, many of the labor leaders are beginning to see the importance of providing a rationale for operations that will go beyond overt political behavior, yet still contribute to political development. It has also become apparent that the early sloganeering, which was efficient as a rudimentary method of political education of the masses in the cause of nationalism, must now give way to a more sustained effort to elicit authentic political responsibility for the good of an established nation.

Education for political responsibility in these states entails a great deal of contributory education. Illiteracy must be combatted, skill training must be instituted, and there must be instruction in citizenship, domestic science, and modern hygiene. For all of this, the union's position in the society is strategic. At present, few of the labor movements are financially able to carry on such programs intensively, but a beginning has been made, especially in experimenting with ways to use the union as an educational and integrative instrument.

In most of the countries I have visited in recent years the unions have been conducting courses of one sort or another and also working to establish health centers and various other social services. There is a valid policy behind these efforts: they can be a partial substitute for the militant, wage-conscious activities frowned upon by parties and governments. But most of the union leaders are aware that the social service activities have an even greater importance. Through such programs, purposefully designed to integrate members of the labor force and their families into the new society, the labor movements will be making a substantial contribution to the establishment of a viable political system.

The labor movements have also been instrumental—and can be more so—in bridging the deep cultural cleavages that mark all the new nations during the period of rapid transition. Being organized essentially around an economic principle, a union is one of the few instruments able to make an impersonal attack on the separations that stem from religious, tribal, and communal traditionalism. In Lebanon, for instance, though the unions must accommodate their operations to the Moslem-Christian split in the society, they are the only organizations with a membership not based exclusively on religious grounds. In Kenya, the unions provide an organizational base that counters tribalism. It was noteworthy that Tom Mboya could be elected to the Kenya Legislative Council in 1960 from a district in Nairobi composed of tribesmen other than his own—and in the face of deliberate opposition attempts to stir up tribal animosity against him.

Examples of the labor union's ability to bring about this kind of integration are legion. In Malaya the plantation workers union is open to all racial and religious groupings, and thus provides one of the few counters to the ethnic separatism that plagues the country.

> . . . a non-communal spirit exists only in labor circles in which the aims and ideals of all groups, no matter what their ethnic origin, are practically identical. This is the greatest blessing bestowed by Malayan trade unionism, which today is both anti-communal and anti-communist. . . . If it can persuade greater numbers of Chinese to join unions and can guard against Communist infiltration, it will have made a more substantial contribution to Malayan unity than any other group.[5]

The Labor Minister of Assam (India) has assessed the union role in promoting national integration as follows:

> One fact looms out large before us: that while the countryside was being convulsed through linguism and regionalism the trade union movement did not lose its head. It kept its integrated character. . . . The question arises how it could be so? The reason is obvious. The working class everywhere is mixed. . . . There is no industry in India worked by only one linguistic group.[6]

In Ceylon, the Trotskyite unions and the LSSP Trotskyite party together constitute one of the few forces on the island that understand the necessity of bridging the religious, linguistic, and ethnic gulf between the Tamils and the Sinhalese. The unions have, however, a limited capacity to attack the problem head on, partly because the prevailing political trends in Ceylon run counter to a too deep commitment by the unions to such a policy.

In sum, most of the unions in Africa and Asia can provide two routes to a better integration of the society. The first demands more resources than are now available to the majority of them; turning a union hall into a classroom and carrying out social service functions

---

[5] Charles Gamba, "Trade Unionism in Malaya," *Far Eastern Survey*, Vol. 23 (February 1954), p. 29.

[6] K. P. Tripathi, "Labour, Trade Union Movement, and Integration," *The Indian Worker* (official journal of the Indian National Trade Union Congress), Vol. 10 (Jan. 29, 1962), p. 8.

In the mid 1950's the Communists, including the AITUC, fed the fires of Indian linguistic separation. More recently, however, S. A. Dange, the head of AITUC, seems to have had second thoughts about the wisdom of this course, which if continued would doubtless lead to the destruction of the AITUC as a national force.

does take money. Outside agencies and organizations could well devote assistance funds to this end. The second route, that of impersonally bridging the cultural and ethnic cleavages in the society, is more dependent than the first on the turn of events outside of union control. The possibilities offered, however, should not be overlooked by outside agencies working with the labor movements.

Countering Communism

The linkage forged in most of the African states between the political forces and the trade unions for the service of nationalism has, in the main, worked against Communist penetration of the labor force. Thus the early union commitment to the ideology of nationalism is an important factor in development.

Before independence, unions in the French colonies absorbed a heavy dose of Communist doctrine and methods because of the predominant role of the Communist-dominated French labor federation (CGT) and the direct affiliation of the colonial unions to this metropole-based confederation. By 1952, however, labor nationalism in both Tunisia and Morocco had triumphed over this domination. Somewhat the same thing happened in French West Africa when, in 1956, Sékou Touré established an autonomous African labor confederation in Guinea and the following year created the General Union of Black African Workers (UGTAN) covering twelve of the territories.

The first two federations established in Kenya soon came under the influence of Communist ideology, and both were duly suppressed by the colonial authorities, one in 1946 and the other in 1950. The present Kenya federation has been dominated by a mix of nationalism and trade unionism. When all of the native political organizations were suppressed during the period of the Mau Mau rebellion, the labor organizations provided the only channel for expression of opinion; under these circumstances, they dealt with a much broader range of issues than unions normally do.

The Communists were quick to see that they could no longer combat nationalism in Africa through their competing union centers. In 1956 they took the step of ordering the centers that were affiliated with the World Federation of Trade Unions (WFTU) to merge with the nationalistic labor centers. Faced with the *fait accompli* of UGTAN in French West Africa, Moscow directly encouraged hard-core Communist unionists to accept it; the same strategy was used for federations in Morocco and elsewhere.

Since the Communist activists who are now working within various African federations have not given up their ultimate goal, they no doubt manage on occasion to shape union policies toward that end. Furthermore, from behind the scenes the WFTU has been trying to encourage the nationalist federations to break their ties with the International Confederation of Free Trade Unions (ICFTU). In Ghana, Guinea (until recently), Mali, and at one time Egypt, the respective federations have furnished a major point of Soviet bloc contact within these states. The Moroccan and the Algerian federations have also maintained extensive contacts with Communist countries. In various parts of Africa the WFTU has skillfully used its sponsorship of the Save Algeria Committee to exert influence.

There is absolutely no doubt, however, that the majority of African unionists are nationalists above all else, and the strength of this single factor impedes the activities of the Communists within their ranks. Most of the union and political leaders are exponents of some brand of socialism, and a number of them are—like Sékou Touré—avowed Marxists. But not all of the Marxists are Communists; when they are not, it is possible for western ideas to gain entry to their organizations and for the Marxist leaders to have at least minimal contact with labor leaders of the West. Such unions still provide a bar to take-overs of the labor force by Communist organizers. Even the most left-leaning leaders do not isolate themselves from other ideological concepts; thus, no matter where the contortions of the present secretary general of the Ghana TUC seem to be heading, he has still retained an adviser from Histadrut in his headquarters.

Both in India and Ceylon labor nationalism has helped to make life less easy for the Communist organizers. In India the INTUC denies them total control of the labor force. In Ceylon, the Ceylon Workers Congress, covering the plantation workers, and the Trotskyite Ceylon Federation of Labor have dominated the scene, keeping Communist union strength to a minimum. A carry-over of this can usually be seen in the general political elections.

In large measure the Trotskyites have pre-empted the left of the political spectrum in Ceylon—a fact which may be of utmost importance to long-term political development. (It so happens that the Trotskyite label is a good deal less revolutionary than it sounds, although certain factions still cling to the original faith.) The more conservative elements on the island perhaps justifiably decry the many strikes, some of which are obviously political. The political strikes, however, are frequently related to the efforts of the non-Communist left to retain dominance in the labor force. When radicalism is endemic, as it is in Ceylon, indigenous "left-wingism" is more tolerable than foreign-supported and anti-national brands. As Walter Galenson points out, "given the attraction for new industrial workers of radical politics as well as radical economics, rendering their organizations illegal may well push worker protest into channels which are fundamentally more subversive to the foundations of a democratic state."[7] Thus, suppression of non-conspiratorial radicalism is not in the ultimate interest of economic stability.

Over all, there is clear evidence that the unions in Africa and Asia which are politically linked to nationalism or socialism, or to both, have served importantly to combat, and sometimes block, Communist attempts to take over segments of the labor force. Even the organizations that still maintain fairly extensive relationships with the Sino-Soviet bloc have been restrained by their national political affiliations from being dominated by the bloc. The outside observers who deplore, per se, political ties between the non-Communist unions and the parties, should ponder this fact, and also consider what the course of unionism and its membership might be if the ties did not exist.

Until development efforts can register more effectively on the societies, such conditions as poor housing, minimal incomes, illiteracy, insecurity within a setting undergoing rapid change, and sometimes the lingering aura—bequeathed by a departed repressive regime—of second-class citizenship will continue to provide the Communist agitators with ready-made opportunities for exploitation. But since the mid 1950's the agitators have increasingly encountered an obstacle—in the ideological commitment of the unions and the union leaders to nationalism and national development. This is the same commitment that, despite certain short-term flirtations with other ideologies and other political forces, usually brings the unions to the support of the nationalist political parties.

Management of Worker Protest

Although the union task of representing the workers' job-related interests frequently appears to be secondary to more directly political

[7] Galenson, ed., *Labor and Economic Development* (Wiley, 1959), pp. 10-11.

tasks, it has been and is being carried on. Furthermore, the job is probably being done as reasonably well as could be expected, given an often fragmented labor force, the limitations placed on collective bargaining, and the social confusion usually attending the establishment of a new political entity. The side effects of success in managing worker protest usually register on the political page of the ledger, and there are many indications that the unions in a good number of localities have made a contribution to political development in this regard.

Obviously, collective bargaining cannot be practiced unilaterally, and before a genuine industrial-relations climate can develop in the new countries, many managers and government officials—as well as union officials and members—need to gain experience in the techniques of the process. In many cases the union approach to bargaining is more sophisticated than that of the employers; when the employers catch up, the way is cleared for greater attention to plant-level problems. Therefore the education of management has often been a part of the general political revolution. In Turkey, Kenya, and Ceylon, where employer representatives now admit frankly to a reappraisal of previous attitudes in regard to unionism, positive steps toward a new industrial-relations climate are being taken to meet the challenge that the new political climate has produced. If a consistent policy of honest bargaining is hewed to by employer interests, the labor organizations will be able to attend more directly to the functions of economic unionism.

Government restraints will probably continue to limit genuinely free collective bargaining for some time to come. What is important now, however, is the establishment of orderly processes by which grievances and disputes can be settled, and the form that this takes matters less than the substance. In most cases, instead of "policing the contract" as a shop steward does in the United States, a union functionary here will be more involved in "policing" and enforcing labor and social protection laws and appearing before government tribunals or intra-party conferences.

The importance to the new governments of having supporters who are capable of managing and directing both political and economic labor protest is manifest if one glances back at past incidents. The anomic and violent upsurges of protest that were characteristic in Africa, dating from Gandhi's famous protest movement in Natal in 1913 and becoming progressively more frequent until 1955, are now less usual. Such methods of registering protest as the episodes of strife in the Rhodesian copper mines in 1950 and the bitter strike of African railroad workers in Southern Rhodesia in 1945—both marked by brutal repression involving numerous deaths—are giving way to fairly disciplined methods under the direction and control of political and union leaders. Recent strikes have tended to be directed at attaining stated objectives and to be contained within the boundaries set by their leaders. As a consequence, violence has been sharply reduced.

Even the general strike of government employees in India in the summer of 1960, a titanic struggle which was only broken when the government brought maximum force into play, resulted in relatively few clashes between troops and strikers. The serious strikes in the port of Ceylon in both 1959 and 1961 were also relatively unmarked by violence. A form of discipline is developing—slowly but genuinely evident—which makes an industrial dispute incomparably easier to handle than, for instance, the demonstrations of much lesser proportions that boil up, undisciplined, about issues relating to communal or language disputes. In part this can be attributed to the growing power of the states, but just as important is the growing capacity of the union leaders to maintain the strikes within prescribed limits.

In Aden during the summer of 1960, many people told me about the capacity of the head of the Aden federation, who is as much a political-nationalist leader as a trade union leader, to impose discipline during tense periods. An official of a refinery, where a ten-week strike had been concluded some months before, expressed his admiration of union discipline: not a single act of sabotage had taken place during the entire strike. He was also impressed by the fact that when the strike concluded (on terms less than favorable to the union) over 95 percent of the workers, many of whom had gone back to their former homes in Yemen, were on the job by at least the second day; this was accomplished despite attempts of a rival nationalist group to keep people off the job.

The political stability that results from trade union success in directing and managing protest must be placed on the plus side of the ledger in discussing labor's contribution to political development. Frequent eruptions, whether they include violence or only the threat of it, destroy the chances of building a viable political system. In the early days of the nationalist struggle and before any mechanism of control was established, such eruptions were inevitable—and in fact were deliberately used from time to time as a weapon against the existing system.

At certain stages, both before and after independence, union leaders have promoted protest and political tension to achieve certain political goals. Now, however, they are concerning themselves more closely with tempering protest and reducing tensions in the work force. This is especially important during the period when ever-increasing numbers of workers are making a first entry into the field of cash employment and at the same time the field of political activity, which can be a heady mixture for the inexperienced. The activities of the Moroccan UMT during the early days of national development, as described below by Douglas E. Ashford, are possibly somewhat untypical in the extent of restraint exercised by the federation, but a good number of labor movements have rendered such services to their states and many more are learning how to do so.

> The contribution of the union to the development of the new country was . . . considerable. Regardless of their natural organizational advantage the workers constituted a crucial group whose expectations and needs had to be represented and fulfilled as much as was possible. More than any other group in Morocco the UMT succeeded in gaining legal and social benefits for its members. . . . Strikes could have been used with political effect, but union leaders exercised restraint. The union leaders understood that no redistribution of existing wealth would noticeably ameliorate the workers' conditions; such a vitally needed change in conditions would require sizeable increases in total national production. . . . [The UMT] relieved considerable tension in the working force and, thereby, [performed] a national service.[8]

Ashford's comment relates in large part to the record of the UMT during the period 1956-59, when it was a part of the Istiqlal complex and working in cooperation with the government. Since its 1959 split with Istiqlal, it has played the role of a responsible opposition, in cooperation with the recently formed political movement, the Union Nationale des Forces Populaires (UNFP). Its demands that the monarchy have a constitutional base and that the long-delayed elections be held have been constructive. However, its challenge to the government is undoubtedly to some extent a part of the usual game of a political opposition that knows it has a red-hot issue to brandish.

The UMT action is an outstanding example of the responsible use of protest, but is not unique. Among the unions now cooperating with their respective governments, there are a number which have an independent base of power and can thus reserve the right to adopt a course

[8] Ashford, *Political Change in Morocco* (Princeton University Press, 1961), pp. 271, 411.

of their own, if, as in Morocco, major political issues remain too long unresolved after independence, or if a restricted elite captures central political power and follows an essentially conservative course.

A Note to Those Interested in Unions Overseas

In writing this assessment of the contributions made by the indigenous labor groups to the development of the new countries, I had very much in mind the groups in the United States—both in the government and in the organized labor movement—that seek to encourage the growth of trade unionism in Africa and Asia. As must be obvious, I do not agree with some of the groups in the extent of their alarm about or disapproval of political unionism. I do agree, however, that in many cases the job-oriented functions of the unions are sometimes unduly subordinated in favor of other functions. And certainly so long as an organization calls itself a trade union the economic function cannot be neglected. On the other hand, practical considerations of the situation demand both something less and something more than aggressive wage-oriented unionism.

This assessment was intended, in part, to suggest that the trade unions' utility in such fields as leadership training, political education, and social integration, all directed at supplying a security buffer to individuals subjected to an accelerated rate of change, may offer an appealing field for study to those interested in the long-term development of the union role. But another intention was to demonstrate, rather categorically, what the labor movements have contributed to total development by means of their often-criticized political commitments—at the same time that they have carried on the more conventional union function, which in its turn assists the building of stable political structures.

CHAPTER NINE

Predictions and Implications

THE POLITICAL PARTY-TRADE UNION MIX discussed in the preceding chapters will probably persist for many more years, although its degree and form will alter according to the turn of events in individual countries. Given the fluidity of the political settings, the availability of a supportive mass organization will continue to be important to the government leaders of most of the young nations. The value of labor movements in this regard is specific: by their very nature they are organizers of both support and protest, and therefore their leadership, if committed to the national cause, can to some extent see to it that mass protest does not get out of hand but takes the disciplined direction necessary to national development.

In those countries where strong centrifugal pressures are forcing the government structure to become highly centralized, and sometimes to border on dictatorship, this specialized capacity of the unions is in some cases bound to make them suspect as competitors to the central political force. Thus the degree of influence and autonomy enjoyed by the labor groups during the independence struggle is due to diminish in the one-party countries—and indeed has already diminished in a few of them—but so far the political involvements of the unions have not noticeably lessened.

In countries where a non-Communist labor movement is in opposition to the central political force, and in others where a number of political currents still compete with each other and with the regime in power at the moment, it is reasonable to assume that the emphasis on political unionism will be part of the picture until the political conflicts are resolved in one way or another. After that, the emphasis may well take a new turn, with the economic function of the unions gradually emerging into more direct view.

For those countries of the Middle East where the "political-maneuver" type of union has been fostered by the unwillingness of the political elites to share power, it is not difficult to visualize popular mass movements being generated by a future round of political shifts. The readiness of such unions to respond to "movementism" was demonstrated during the early days of the 1958 revolution in Iraq, when the Communists were highly successful in generating a mass organization. The number of trade unions jumped from a mere handful to hundreds, with a total of perhaps 250,000 so-called members on call for riots and strikes in support of CP goals.[1]

To venture the above predictions is the more possible because, for some time to come, two factors common to most of the countries will continue to reinforce the course that trade unionism has taken. First, industrialization is still so minimal or, at best, spotty that targets to be aimed at by the economic functions of unionism will remain limited. At present and probably for a number of years, worker benefits cannot be extracted directly from most employers, since there is really little "fat" to spare and the national leaders will be concerned primarily with capital investment.

The second factor is the degree of social repression that prevailed in a given country prior to independence. If a population had in the main been denied even the rudiments of social justice by the former government, the stage is set for demands for sweeping social and economic change. And even when repression was less—or was applied quite politely by an enlightened colonial power—most of those subjected to it will also clamor for change, once the elixir of independence has been tasted. The unions are involved in the type of change demanded and are usually its enthusiastic sponsors. But the union leadership is in general convinced that the new economic and social goals must still be attained through political means.

It is obvious that the labor movements of these regions are not always on the side of the angels. This is all the more reason for the Americans and other westerners who are interested in the political and economic development of the new states to examine the essential elements of labor's political role very specifically when planning pro-

---

[1] In 1960 the unions came under administrative control of the Iraq government and the hold of the Communists seemingly was broken.

grams and policies designed to further modernization of the unions. In many instances an analyst is likely to find that a union's influence within a political complex is deleterious. The labor leaders may be exploiting their power position to the point of overwhelming the political leaders, who may then retaliate by using the only weapon left to them—repressive extremism—not only against the unions but also against all of the other interest groups that originally provided the independence movement with its broad base. In many other cases the analyst will discover that a labor movement is a progressive and dynamic element within the political arena and provides a constructive way of introducing a vital segment of mass society to citizenship.

The political union can make any one of a number of impacts on the political scene. When an analysis in depth shows that a labor organization's political operations are menacing the development of national unity, a certain type of program planning is indicated for the outside labor adviser. Quite another approach is needed when both the union and the party leaderships are progressive and sensibly determined to make the partnership work; and still another when a dynamic union is being restrained unduly by an increasingly centralized government. The variations on the theme are many and subtle—but well worth attention.

The next section deals with "implications" rather than the more formal "recommendations" sometimes proffered to conclude a study. The self-assumed American task of encouraging the growth of sound, viable trade unionism in the emerging countries is so big and many-sided that categorical recommendations by any one man would be presumptuous. Further, at this state of the art there is essentially only one recommendation to be made: that the present realities of labor's role in Africa and Asia should be studied closely, and on a scale broader than a single-country analysis, by the labor specialists, internationalists, political scientists, economists, sociologists, anthropologists, and any others who are—or ought to be—concerned with this field.

This book has been an attempt to demonstrate the necessity of such a recommendation, and perhaps it should therefore be termed a pilot project, offered to stimulate similar but much more extensive studies. In any case, in the paragraphs that follow, the main points of the study are stressed briefly and their significance is considered.

Implications

1. In most of the developing countries of Africa and Asia, the trade unions are a part of the mechanism that carries on the day-to-day political processes of a nation. Therefore, whether their role is supportive of a political force currently in power or, for reasons valid or invalid, in opposition to it, they are frequently able to influence the course of political and economic development by various means. The economic function of collective bargaining is one of these means—but at present only one.

When the unions are linked to a sound political force, they usually reinforce its soundness and its progressive tendencies and contribute a dynamism that accrues in part from their representational mass base. Their management of worker protest provides some degree of protection against the subversive elements that exploit the shockingly low standards of living still evident. And in many cases, union membership is the sole factor that gives the new and often bewildered urban worker any feeling of belonging to the society that is evolving.

Labor participation in the politics of these countries is at present an established reality. That the consequence of this may at times not be salutary for a given political movement or labor movement does not lessen but increases the need for western labor advisers to understand the significance of this role of the unions. Dismissal or disregard of the significance sharply diminishes the chances of understanding political events and combinations in any of the countries, and thus of assisting the eventual development of a stable trade unionism.

There especially needs to be an understanding of the many instances where breaking the political tie would court disaster. In India, for example, the INTUC's effectiveness as a collective bargaining instrument is undoubtedly much reduced as a result of its connections with the Congress Party. But, under the present circumstances at least, without the party tie INTUC probably could not survive—and there is no gainsaying the union's value in denying control of the total labor force to the Communists. Perhaps even more important is the counterweight provided by the INTUC to certain extremely conservative elements within the Congress Party. Lacking such a counterweight, the party could become increasingly unrepresentative of the mass electorate, with possible serious consequences to political stability.

In any of the young nations, the outcome of a struggle between Communists and non-Communists may depend on the effectiveness of the labor arm of a nationalist movement as a propaganda agent for its political partner. Thus the political strike may possibly have great value in enlisting the masses on the side of the more democratic political force—and collective bargaining, aside from its inherent value, can be a major tool in winning political loyalty. An American labor adviser may not wish to encourage such tactics—but he should be able to acknowledge the necessity, and possibly the virtue, of their employment under certain circumstances. Logic suggests that unhealthy political situations can best be challenged through political means. Inasmuch as a labor movement is already one of the elements in the political system, and usually one of the more progressive, it is a useful conveyance for the part of the challenge that falls within its specialized province.

2. An understanding of mass movements and of the ideologies that motivate them is a first requirement for Americans working in the field, especially since the idiom has been essentially foreign to the present, and much of the past, American experience. The forays of the IWW and the Populist activities of the People's Party both had some likeness to mass movement operations, but because they were never more than the protests of minority groups, they were a far cry from what is now happening in Asia and Africa.

The mass movement union in the new countries must operate across a broad base of functions. It is important for the outside labor adviser to know both the depth of commitment to the national cause and the competence with which a given union carries out each one of its functions. The knowledge provides a basis for determining, case by case, whether a union can be counted on as a dependable ally of a sound political force. The adviser could, for example, play an important part in bringing together political and labor units to cooperate in building a progressive non-Communist party.

Such knowledge is also essential in planning programs that will be realistic aids to union development. They must of course contain a heavy component of activities related to the economic function, because training and practice in this area are badly needed. But a program in trade union leadership, for example, would limit its usefulness if it did not reflect the probability that some of its participants have important political responsibilities, or may eventually have them. Effective programs cannot be developed in isolation from the general social context in which the participants must operate, nor when they are not based on a clear understanding of the type of political alliance a union has at present or is likely to have in a foreseeable future. When a labor movement is found to be more dynamic than the political movement of which it is a part, it might even be useful, in certain circumstances, to gear programs toward a healthier development for the total movement rather than for the trade unions alone. In any case, American personnel who are to work with the unions in these countries ought to be selected especially for their capacity to be aware of the social contexts they will find, and then trained further in the specific skills needed to operate within these contexts.

3. It can be taken for granted that the successful and dynamic nationalist movements in countries where political competition is limited will expect continued cooperation from the labor organizations which worked at their side during the drive for independence. But in the present flux, even a successful government may suspect that any other force with a power base is a threatening rival. The conflict is compounded by the unions' desire to press for benefits for their membership—an effort that frequently runs counter to the over-all needs of economic development. Sooner or later the government may move to bring the unions under some degree of control. Inevitably, the question of unions' rights will arise, as further tensions develop.

This is a difficult issue for an outsider. On one hand, his professional commitment is to encourage the development of trade unions, not as captives, but as viable institutions. On the other hand, he may recognize that in some cases it is reasonable to expect the new governments to exercise a fairly stiff centralized authority until a workable national consensus has been reached.

How free the unions should be—or can be—under these circumstances is highly debatable, and certainly cannot be resolved in the abstract. Even when subject to restraints, however, they usually retain their ability to apply some degree of pressure on the political system— because they serve as a reception center for those making the transition from rural to urban life, because they have contact with the masses on a continuing basis, and because they are intimately involved with the process of modernizing the economic system. In those societies where genuine mass parties are developing, or may develop, the need of the political leaders to maintain a vibrant quality in the movement will afford some protection to the unions, even though for the time being they will fall far short of being independent.

There is a possible long-view solution to the dilemma. Direct intervention by outsiders in an already tightened conflict would obviously do more harm than good. But the existence of such situations and the possibility that others will arise suggest that Americans in the field might find it profitable to discuss—as part of a "permanent dialogue" —the separation of functions seen in the Scandinavian union-party relationships, which I believe offers a hope of a realistic and viable system that might be applicable here. But until thorough investigation of this relationship pattern, as well as of other possible courses, results in an inspired method for relating them to the environment of the new nations, outside advisers should not lightly consider the disruption of existing relationships between the unions and their political partners.

Even when undue restraints are being imposed on the unions, the fact of the relationship persists, and provides a base on which can possibly be built in the future a workable form more in keeping with democracy. Furthermore, when an alignment breaks up and the labor federation goes into opposition to its former nationalist partner, the union is exposed to the threat of increased Communist influence within its ranks, which might culminate in complete Communist domination.

Strong unions can fend off the threat, especially if their commitment to the nationalist cause has not been lessened by the disruption of the former relationship. Not all unions are this strong, however. And when the opposition tactics of one of the weaker sort fail to extract benefits that will at least partially satisfy the growing demands of its members for better living standards, the work force it represents becomes an easy target for Communist exploitation.

4. In the countries where political competition exists, some of the nationalist unions have chosen to affiliate with one or another of the parties that are in opposition to the government. Their commitment to the ideology of nationalism is not changed thereby—and may in their own view be enhanced. Americans sometimes suggest that union mergers in such situations would be an advantage on several counts, and especially in presenting a united opposition front against the Communists. But a merger cannot reasonably be expected to happen where there is no political basis for it and where competing ideological issues are at stake.

In India, for example, a merger of the non-Communist unions would wipe out part of the base support of the Praja Socialist Party, which represents a loyal opposition to the government. To promote political stability in India through assisting the healthy development of a loyal opposition seems more important in the long run than uniting the INTUC and the Socialist HMS in the name of building an anti-Communist labor front. Moreover, to submerge the HMS in this fashion would polarize the work force and thereby probably add to the strength of the Communist AITUC.

5. "Radicalism" in varying degrees has been and probably will continue to be the mark of most of the developing countries with mass movements and mass parties.[2] It has been demonstrated many times that a gradualist politics of the center has little merit in the eyes of the mass electorates which have come into being at such an early stage of national development.

The labor movements within each country are a natural and major source of these tendencies. Not all of the unions are "radical," but within each political complex they usually stand at the left of the political spectrum, making demands for better living conditions, more housing, more social protection, more this and more that. The INTUC, for example, is not a radical organization; on the other hand, it is more radical than are some other elements of the Congress Party, and it is pulled to the left by the competition of the Socialist HMS and the Communist AITUC. Even the unions in Egypt, which are not strong power centers, by the very fact of their existence provide impetus to the continuing demands for sweeping economic and social reform.

The endemic radicalism of most of the parties and the inherent drive to the left of the union leaders, while perhaps uncomfortable to live with, are not always undesirable. This is particularly true if a union is allied with a political force capable of harnessing the energy and utilizing the constructive possibilities offered through union channels. The unions of the non-Communist left, as a force for modernization and development in societies with built-in obstacles to change, are in many instances promoting the same type of change that the West itself desires for the new countries. For that reason alone, Americans must learn to work with them.

"Work with" is not the same thing as accepting the point of view of the nationalist and socialist union leaders on all issues. They have

[2] The term "radicalism" is put in quotes here to indicate that in general the connotation given it by an average voter in the United States is quite different from the meaning that would be intended by his counterpart in, say, Kenya, Israel, or Norway. The former would be apt to find it an alarming word, the latter probably not, for it seems to be true that a good part of the world's electorate stands to the left of the American electorate.

no corner on wisdom, but we should be able to comprehend the pressures that have molded the point of view and to understand that these men want our technology but are doubtful of some of our values. It has been made clear on numerous occasions that a good many of them do not at present consider the social and economic systems of the United States notably worthy of emulation. American labor advisers have, then, an ambassadorial job to do, which might well begin with the establishment of sound working relations with the party and union leaders of the non-Communist left. Somewhere along the way a certain amount of mutual trust might emerge.

6. There are still several countries in the Middle East and in Southeast Asia where trade unions are either not tolerated, or under such controls that they are no more than a potential. These are societies especially plagued by low living standards, social imbalance, and political repression. In the rare cases where unions are allowed legal status, they become objects of solicitude from important figures in the political opposition; should a major fault shake the central political structure, it can almost be taken for granted that the clusters of labor groups will join an opposition movement seeking drastic political change. It is also quite possible, during a period of political gestation in any one of the countries in this group, that some of the unions themselves will form the core of an opposition movement.

Until labor organizations in these several countries acquire some political influence by one means or another, their potential as economic trade unions will be very low, yet if they do join an opposition movement they will become increasingly political. The American decision of whether or not to assist groups that are emerging into intensive political activity in this way will have to depend on the nature of the political alliance they make. But if assistance is given, its programs should take into account both the economic and the political strivings of the unions involved.

7. Giving recognition to the politics of labor still leaves substantial room for programs designed to improve the techniques the trade unions need to institutionalize their economic function of representing the worker and protecting his interests. However, the programs could well be three-pronged in their approach, since both management and government require education in this and similar fields.

Government administrators on various levels need instruction in the procedures of collective bargaining and of internal union operations. They should also be trained in the operation of labor exchanges, the administration of social security legislation, and so on. And there is a pressing need for governments to make manpower assessments in relation to their future development projects; from these it can be determined what kind and quantity of education and skill-training will be necessary for the work force before specific projects can be set in motion.

Management is particularly in need of assistance in the training of personnel to carry on labor relations. Political changes have paved the way for a change in attitudes toward unionism and thus opened up the opportunity for building an objective approach to employee relations. Although there is still hostility to labor organizations in many quarters, each year sees an increasing number of employers become more flexible, but many of them know little or nothing about the internal dynamics of trade unions. A group of Asian businessmen with whom I spent some time in 1959 very evidently wanted to learn; they wanted to know, for instance, why union leaders took stances under given sets of circumstances, and what a trade union looked like from the inside. They had begun to realize, they said, that only when they understood the play of forces within a labor organization would they be prepared to carry on an orderly pattern of industrial relations.

As for the trade unions themselves, many have reached a point at which the leaders must focus greater attention on developing wider sources of leadership, especially at the local level; unifying the membership; systematizing internal administration; and increasing their skills for maintaining collective relationships with management. All of this is necessary if the unions are to become firm institutions.

It is also necessary if they are to carry out their part in helping solve what looms as a pressing social problem for the near future. All of the new governments recognize that an increase in literacy is a necessary key to progress. Yet this achievement is bound at first to breed or heighten radical tendencies in the politically unsophisticated. For the labor force especially, the ability to read will open a vast new field of impressions, ideas, desires. When an increase in educational opportunities far outpaces an increase in economic opportunities and improvement in social status, it is axiomatic that the beckonings of extremist politics—whether of the right or of the left—may become highly persuasive. A trade union can partly counter this seduction when its cohesiveness and job-related activities demonstrate to the worker that his affiliation with it is a firm two-way pact and that the leadership is not only aware of his wants but working to perfect the machinery which will satisfy at least some of them.

In most of the new states of Asia and Africa the achievement of an industrial economy that can employ and grant benefits to any significant proportion of the potential labor forces is far in the future. It could be even more delayed, or possibly prevented, if national development efforts do not also include the building of other social institutions which will (1) guard against the danger of too much political power concentrated in too few special-interest centers and (2) assure a reasonable measure of economic and social justice throughout a nation.

The labor movements which helped to win independence and which are still responsibly committed to the cause of nationalism and betterment of social conditions are well equipped to assist in the building of such institutions. In part this capacity resides in their traditional function of protecting the rights of the worker. In larger part, it stems from the politically-oriented awareness of the union leaders that a worker's job rights will never be firmly established until there is no question of his wider rights as a citizen of a viable society.

For some time to come the prospects for success or failure of the governments' nation-building efforts will be balanced on a delicate scale. The trade unions are only one of the social components that will influence the balance, but their consequential political role gives them a weight few other interest groups have. In one country or another the operations of an irresponsible labor movement, whether partner or opponent, could tip the scale toward failure. Those of a responsible movement could help insure success. And one probable indication that success has been attained will be a clearer separation of trade union functions from those of a political party—not because the political partnerships have been dissolved, but because other special-interest groups will have been established to help carry on the governance of a nation.

Bibliography

BOOKS AND MANUSCRIPTS

Almond, Gabriel A., and Coleman, James S., eds. *The Politics of the Developing Areas.* Princeton: Princeton University Press, 1960.

Ashford, Douglas E. *Political Change in Morocco.* Princeton: Princeton University Press, 1961.

Bennett, George, and Rosberg, Carl G. *The Kenyatta Election: Kenya 1960-1961.* New York: Oxford University Press, 1961.

Davison, R. B. "African Labour Studies of (I) Migrancy and (II) Industrial Relations Within a Factory in the Gold Coast." Washington: Library of Congress (microfilm).

Duverger, Maurice. *Political Parties.* Translated by Barbara and Robert North. New York: Wiley (revised edition), 1959.

Elkan, Walter. *Migrants and Proletarians.* New York: Oxford University Press, 1960.

Estey, J. A. *Revolutionary Syndicalism.* London: P. S. King, 1913.

Fisher, S. N., ed. *Social Forces in the Middle East.* Ithaca: Cornell University Press, 1955.

Galenson, Walter, ed. *Labor and Economic Development.* New York: Wiley, 1959.

Ghosh, Subratesh. *Trade Unionism in the Underdeveloped Countries.* Calcutta: Bookland Private, 1960.

Haldar, M. K., and Ghosh, Robin, eds. *Problems of Economic Growth.* (Report of a Seminar held in Tokyo, April 1957, sponsored by the Congress for Cultural Freedom.) New Delhi: Prabhakar Padhye, 1960.

Harrison, Selig S. *India, the Most Dangerous Decades.* Princeton: Princeton University Press, 1960.

Hodgkin, Thomas. *African Political Parties.* Harmondsworth, Middlesex: Penguin Books, 1961.

——. *Nationalism in Colonial Africa.* London: Fredrick Muller, 1956.

Holland, William L., ed. *Asian Nationalism and the West.* New York: Macmillan, 1953.

Hoselitz, Bert F., ed. *The Progress of Underdeveloped Areas.* Chicago: University of Chicago Press, 1952.

Kassalow, Everett M., ed. *National Labor Movements in the Postwar World.* (Papers of the National Institute of Labor Education Research Seminar on Comparative Labor Movements.) Evanston: Northwestern University Press, 1963.

Kerr, Clark, and others. *Industrialism and Industrial Man.* Cambridge: Harvard University Press, 1960.

138

Kornhauser, William. *The Politics of Mass Society*. Glencoe, Illinois: Free Press, 1959.

Lipset, Seymour Martin. *Political Man*. Garden City: Doubleday, 1960.

Moore, Wilbert E., and Feldman, Arnold S., eds. *Labor Commitment and Social Change in Developing Areas*. New York: Social Science Research Council, 1960.

Myers, Charles A. *Labor Problems in the Industrialization of India*. Cambridge: Harvard University Press, 1958.

Orr, Charles A. "Labor and Nationalism in Africa." Unpublished manuscript, Roosevelt University, 1962 (hectographed).

Park, Richard L., and Tinker, Irene, eds. *Leadership and Political Institutions in India*. Princeton: Princeton University Press, 1959.

Roper, J. I. *Labour Problems in West Africa*. Harmondsworth, Middlesex: Penguin Books, 1958.

Saposs, David. *Left-Wing Unionism*. New York: International Publishers, 1926.

Shils, Edward, *et al*. *Democracy in the New States*. (Papers of a Seminar held in Rhodes, November 1959, sponsored by the Congress for Cultural Freedom.) New Delhi: Prabhakar Padhye, 1959.

Smythe, Hugh H. and Mabel M. *The New Nigerian Elite*. Stanford: Stanford University Press, 1960.

Sombart, Werner. *Socialism and the Social Movement in the 19th Century*. Translated by Anson P. Atterbury. New York: Putnam's, 1898.

Tedjasukmana, Iskandar. *The Political Character of the Indonesian Trade Union Movement*. Monograph Series, Modern Indonesia Project. Ithaca: Cornell University, 1958 (multilith).

Waldstein, Nan S. *The Indigenous African Trade Union Movements of Nigeria, the Federation of Rhodesia and Nyasaland, French West Africa, and the Belgian Congo*. Cambridge: Center for International Studies, Massachusetts Institute of Technology, 1960 (hectographed).

Wallerstein, Immanuel. *Africa: The Politics of Independence*. New York: Vintage Books, 1961.

Warmington, W. A. *A West African Trade Union*. Nigerian Institute of Social and Economic Research Publications. New York: Oxford University Press, 1960.

Weiner, Myron. *Party Politics in India*. Princeton: Princeton University Press, 1957.

Wriggins, W. Howard. *Ceylon: Dilemmas of a New Nation*. Princeton: Princeton University Press, 1960.

PERIODICALS

Annals of the American Academy of Political and Social Science, "Agrarian Societies in Transition," Vol. 305, May 1956, entire issue.

——, "Contemporary Africa: Trends and Issues," Vol. 298, March 1955, entire issue.

——, "Current Issues in International Labor Relations," Vol. 310, March 1957, entire issue.

Apter, David E. "The Role of Traditionalism in the Political Modernization of Ghana and Uganda." *World Politics*, Vol. 13, October 1960, pp. 45-68.

Ashford, Douglas E. "Labor Politics in a New Nation." *Western Political Quarterly*, Vol. 13, June 1960, pp. 312-331.

Becu, Omer. "Free Trade Unions in Developing Countries." *Free Labour World* (official journal of the ICFTU), No. 133, July 1961, pp. 276-280.

Beling, Willard A. "Political Trends in Arab Labor." *Middle East Journal*, Vol. 15, Winter 1961, pp. 29-39.

Chao, Kuo-Chun. "Agricultural Laborers in India." *Far Eastern Survey*, Vol. 26, January 1957, pp. 24-31.

Chidzero, B.T.G. "African Nationalism in East and Central Africa." *International Affairs*, Vol. 36, October 1960, pp. 464-475.

Cooper, Harold. "Political Preparedness for Self-Government." *Annals of the American Academy of Political and Social Science*, Vol. 306, July 1956, pp. 71-77.

Deutsch, Karl W. "Social Mobilization and Political Development." *American Political Science Review*, Vol. 15, September 1961, pp. 493-514.

Fisher, Paul. "The Economic Role of Unions in Less-Developed Areas." *Monthly Labor Review*, Vol. 84, September 1961, pp. 951-956.

Gamba, Charles. "Labour and Labour Parties in Malaya." *Pacific Affairs*, Vol. 31, June 1958, pp. 117-130.

——. "Trade Unionism in Malaya." *Far Eastern Survey*, Vol. 23, February 1954, pp. 28-30.

Gomberg, William. "The Future of Collective Bargaining." *The Nation*, Vol. 194, January 20, 1962, pp. 56-61.

Harris, C. C., and Nyerere, Julius. "Tanganyika Today: I. The Background; II. The Nationalist View." *International Affairs*, Vol. 36, January 1960, pp. 35-47.

Harrison, Selig S. "The Challenge to Indian Nationalism." *Foreign Affairs*, Vol. 34, July 1956, pp. 620-636.

Hochschild, Harold K. "Labor Relations in Northern Rhodesia." *Annals of the American Academy of Political and Social Science*, Vol. 306, July 1956, pp. 43-49.

Huxley, Elspeth. "The Next-to-Last Act in Africa." *Foreign Affairs*, Vol. 39, July 1961, pp. 655-669.

James, Ralph. "Politics and Trade Unions in India." *Far Eastern Survey*, Vol. 27, March 1958, pp. 41-45.

Kannappan, Subbiah. "The Tata Steel Strike: Some Dilemmas of Industrial Relations in a Developing Economy." *Journal of Political Economy*, Vol. 67, October 1959, pp. 489-507.

Kraft, Joseph. "Settler Politics in Algeria." *Foreign Affairs*, Vol. 39, July 1961, pp. 591-600.

Laqueur, Walter Z. "Communism and Nationalism in Tropical Africa." *Foreign Affairs*, Vol. 39, July 1961, pp. 610-621

Lichtblau, George E. "The Politics of Trade Union Leadership in Southern Asia." *World Politics,* Vol. 7, October 1954, pp. 85-101.

von der Mehden, Fred R. "Marxism and Early Islamic Nationalism." *Political Science Quarterly,* Vol. 73, September 1958, pp. 335-351.

Mehta, Asoka. "The Mediating Role of the Trade Union in Under Developed Countries." *Economic Development and Cultural Change,* Vol. 6, October 1957, pp. 16-23.

———. "The Political Mind of India." *Foreign Affairs,* Vol. 35, July 1957, pp. 679-688.

Neufeld, Maurice F. "The Inevitability of Political Unionism in Underdeveloped Countries: Italy, the Exemplar." *Industrial and Labor Relations Review,* Vol. 13, April 1960, pp. 363-386.

Ornati, Oscar A. "Indian Trade Unions Since Independence." *Far Eastern Survey,* Vol. 23, August 1954, pp. 113-122.

———. "Problems of Indian Trade Unionism." *Annals of the American Academy of Political and Social Science,* Vol. 310, March 1957, pp. 151-161.

Pauker, Guy J. "The Role of Political Organizations in Indonesia." *Far Eastern Survey,* Vol. 27, September 1958, pp. 129-142.

Perham, Margery. "White Minorities in Africa." *Foreign Affairs,* Vol. 37, July 1959, pp. 637-648.

Rimmer, Douglas K. "The New Industrial Relations in Ghana." *Industrial and Labor Relations Review,* Vol. 14, January 1961, pp. 206-226.

Roberts, B. C. "Trade Unions in Colonial Dependencies." *British Affairs,* Vol. 4, March 1960, pp. 12-15.

Schacter, Ruth. "Single-Party Systems in West Africa." *American Political Science Review,* Vol. 55, June 1961, pp. 294-307.

Shils, Edward. "The Intellectuals in the Political Development of the New States." *World Politics,* Vol. 12, April 1960, pp. 329-368.

Singh, Jitendra. "Communism in Kerala." *Political Quarterly,* Vol. 31, April-June 1960.

Skinner, Elliott P. "Traditional and Modern Patterns of Succession to Political Office Among the Mossi of the Voltaic Republic." *Journal of Human Relations,* Vol. 8, Spring-Summer 1960, pp. 394-406.

Smythe, Hugh H. and Mabel M. "Black Africa's New Power Elite." *South Atlantic Quarterly,* Vol. 59, Winter 1960, pp. 13-23.

Sturmthal, Adolph. "Unions and Economic Development." *Economic Development and Cultural Change,* Vol. 8, January 1960, pp. 199-205.

Touré, Sékou. "The Republic of Guinea." *International Affairs,* Vol. 36, April 1960, pp. 168-173.

Trachtman, Lester N. "The Labor Movement of Ghana: A Study in Political Unionism." *Economic Development and Cultural Change,* Vol. 10, January 1962, Part 1, pp. 183-200.

Tripathi, K. P. "Labour, Trade Union Movement, and Integration." *The Indian Worker* (official journal of the Indian National Trade Union Congress), Vol. 10, January 29, 1962, p. 8.

Tucker, Robert C. "Towards a Comparative Politics of Movement-Regimes." *American Political Science Review,* Vol. 55, June 1961, pp. 281-289.

Whitehead, Sir Edgar. "Southern Rhodesia." *International Affairs,* Vol. 36, April 1960, pp. 188-196.

GOVERNMENT PUBLICATIONS,
PAMPHLETS, REFERENCE MATERIALS, AND SPEECHES

Bowen, Walter. *Colonial Trade Unions*. (Research Series No. 167.) London: Fabian Publications, 1954.

Bratteli, Trygve. Address to 1957 Convention of the Norwegian Federation of Labor, in *Protokoll Over Kongressen* (official record of the Convention), p. 26.

Dange, S. A. *On the Indian Trade Union Movement*. Bombay: Communist Party Publication, 1952.

Ghana, Office of the Government Statistician. *Quarterly Digest of Statistics,* Vol. 9, September 1960.

Indian Communist Party Documents, 1930-1956. Published for the Democratic Research Service and the Institute of Pacific Relations. Bombay: Kanada Press, 1957.

International Labour Organisation. *African Labour Survey*. Geneva: ILO, 1958.

——. *Labour Survey of North Africa*. Geneva: ILO, 1960.

Kenya, Colony and Protectorate of. *Labour Department Annual Report, 1959*. Nairobi: Government Printer, 1960.

Kimble, George H. T. *Tropical Africa* (2 vols.). New York: Twentieth Century Fund, 1960.

Nigeria, Eastern Region. *Department of Labour Annual Report, 1957-58*. Enugu: Government Printer, 1958.

Nigeria, Federation of. *Report of the Board of Inquiry into the Trade Dispute Between the Elder Dempster Lines, Limited, and the Nigerian Union of Seamen, June 1959*. Lagos: Government Printer, 1959.

Segal, Ronald. *Political Africa: A Who's Who of Personalities and Parties*. New York: Praeger, 1961.

U.S. Department of Labor, Bureau of Labor Statistics. *Labor in India* (Report No. 188). Washington: Government Printing Office, 1961.

——. *Labor Law and Practice in Ceylon*. Washington: Government Printing Office, 1962.

U.S. Foreign Policy Study, No. 10, *Ideology and Foreign Affairs*. Prepared for the Senate Committee on Foreign Relations by the Harvard University Center for International Affairs. Washington: Government Printing Office, 1960.

Index

Aden Trade Union Congress (ATUC), 24, 28, 77, 124

Adoula, Cyrille, 115

Africa (*see also* names of countries): Communism in, 44, 120-22; leadership in, 114-16; nationalism, 64-65, 69-79; one-party systems, 107-08; post-independence problems, 43, 46, 55, 102-03; social imbalance, 60-63; strikes in, 123-24; tribal relationships, 15, 48; work force, 56, 58-60

Africa, trade unions in: Characteristics of, 5, 13, 14, 18-36, 81-82, 130; Communist, 120-21; economic unionism, 75-78; lack of economic unionism, 56-57; origins, 65-69; political unionism, 7-8, 10, 16, 51-52, 53, 91-92, 96-98; possibilities for, 119-20; U.S. interest in, 126-37

Alexander, Robert J., 12n

Algeria, 13, 69, 121

All Indian Trade Union Congress (AITUC): Competition with INTUC, 104, 107, 134; leadership, 27, 115; "opposition" role, 51; political orientation, 23, 35, 87, 109, 119n

Almond, Gabriel A., 12n

Arab Trade Unions, Confederation of, 28

Ashford, Douglas E., 24n, 45n, 125

Asia (*see also* names of countries): Civil liberties, 47-48; nationalism, 43-44, 64-65, 69-72, 79; post-independence problems, 46, 55, 114; social imbalance, 60-63; unskilled labor, 59-60

Asia, trade unions in: Characteristics of, 5, 17-36, 81-82, 130; economic unionism, 75-78; origins, 66-68; political unionism, 7-8, 10, 16, 51, 53, 92, 96-99,

135; possibilities for, 119-20; restraints, on, 107; U.S. interest in, 129-37

Ba, Abdoulaye, 115

Bakunin, Mikhail, 39

Ben Seddik, Mahjoub, 28

Bennett, George, 45n

Benton, William, 5

Berg, Elliot, 32n, 58n, 67

Beyioku, Olujimi A.F., 15

Blake, Donald J., 101n

Blanksten, George I., 12n

Bombay dock workers union, 24

Bowen, Walter, 68n

Bratteli, Trygve, 101n

Calcutta dock workers union, 27

Cameroons (British), 76-77

Cameroun (French), 20, 45

Capital accumulation vs. consumption, 105-07

Ceylon: Bank employees, 32, 93; government workers, 33; labor, 103-14; strikes, 92-94, 122, 124; Trotskyite parties, 27, 83, 119; wage boards, 34

Ceylon, unions in: Collective bargaining, 123; Communist, 28, 87, 93, 121; Federation of Labor, 27, 83, 87, 121; Government Clerical Service, 24, 27; leadership in, 27; Mercantile, 27; multiple unionism, 14, 18-19, 23, 49, 78, 90; political unionism, 12; Trotskyite, 27, 51, 83, 87, 119, 121; unifying role, 119; Workers Congress (CWC), 24, 25-26, 27, 121

Choudhury, H. R., 27

Civil liberties, 47-48

Cole, G.D.H., 66, 67n

143